A Bi

Reflections

Heather.
I am praying
for you.
Enjoy!

Patty

A 90-Day Devotional and Journal
for People Who Love Birds

Outdoor Devotional Series

A Bird Lover's Reflections

Patty Mondore

North Wind Publishing
Brewer, Maine

North Wind Publishing
P.O. Box 3655
Brewer, ME 04412
northwindpublishing.com

10 9 8 7 6 5 4 3 2 1

ISBN 978-0-9895689-3-7

Library of Congress Control Number: 2014956277

Bookstores/Giftshops: Bulk ordering is available. Contact
info@northwindpublishing.com. Also available through
Ingram and Spring Arbor Distributors.

Dedication

It is such a privilege and joy to be able to dedicate this book to my bird-loving dad, George Wilson. He has been an inspiration to me in so many ways, throughout my entire life. Having just turned 90, he still enjoys watching birds at his feeders. But more importantly, he has always been, and continues to be an example to me of a deep faith and a love of God that can see me through whatever life throws at me. Dad, I hope you enjoy your daughter's bird-loving reflections. I love you! Patty

Publisher's Note

. . . and let birds fly above the earth . . . (Gen. 1:20)

A Bird Lover's Reflections by Patty Mondore is one book in a series of devotionals for people who love the outdoors. One summer I completed a "Bucket List" item. After waiting to go for many years, I finally made it to Machais Seal Island in Maine to photograph the Atlantic Puffins that nest on the island (that's a puffin in the photo above.) God sure has a sense of humor to create such a beautiful but awkward bird. Puffins live at sea most of the year and are expert divers but on land, puffins waddle when they walk and make a lot of crash landings. Some locals call them the clowns of the ocean.

    A Bird Lover's Reflections is a 90-day Devotional and Journal to help you with your bible study and meditations. Each day starts with a beautiful black and white bird photo and bible verse. *Winging Through the Word* steers you toward portions of the bible you should read that day while *Thoughts on the Fly* are the author's personal experiences enjoying birds and where she relates that experience to biblical teachings. The *Birder's Journal* is an area for the reader to write down personal thoughts for the day, so this book becomes a keepsake journal. May God bless you and yours.

JANET ROBBINS, Publisher

Introduction

Devotions in Nature

A study was done a few years ago by the U.S. Fish and Wild-life Service indicating that one in every five Americans enjoys the hobby of bird watching. The report claimed that 48 million people considered themselves bird watchers. I'm definitely one of them. My husband and I started with a single bird feeder when we bought our first home and have somehow expanded our collection to about eight feeders at home, four or five at camp, with an additional assortment of bird houses in both locations.

Why do so many of us watch birds? I'm sure you would get a different answer from just about anyone you ask. They are beautiful, accessible, and fascinating to watch. Plus, observing them in the natural world helps draw our attention away from the stresses around us. Watching water fowl takes us to the water's edge which offers its own added component of beauty and wonder. Learning to identify some of the different bird songs is more entertaining (at least for me) than knowing every song on the Billboard Hot 100. And being able to set up feeding stations where our various feathered friends can come and freely dine, gives me a sense of satisfaction that is hard to describe.

But I think that the main reason I find such joy in watching my little bird friends is that they continually direct my focus back to their Creator. I am convinced that God speaks to us, and reveals attributes of himself to us, through his natural world. The birds at our feeders and in our trees are a constant reminder to me that God is good, that he is in control even in a world that sometimes seems to be spinning out of control, and that he will faithfully provide for all who put their trust in him.

Jesus must have spent some of his time watching the birds he created. He mentioned them repeatedly in his parables and used them as illustrations to teach his followers about life, faith, and their heavenly Father. He told his listeners: "Look at the birds of the air: they neither sow nor reap nor gather into barns, and yet your heavenly Father feeds them. Are you not of more value than they?" (Matthew 6:26). And so you are!

Since you have picked up this book you are presumably a bird watcher, too. Come join me on this short flight into God's amazing kingdom of birds as well as through his written Word at the same time. See if, like me, you find yourself being drawn closer along the way to the One who provided us with both.

PATTY MONDORE

A Bird Lover's

Reflections

1. Every Winged Bird

Morning Song: *And God said, "Let the waters swarm with swarms of living creatures, and let birds fly above the earth across the expanse of the heavens."*
(Genesis 1:20)

Winging Through the Word
Read: Genesis 1:1-21

Thoughts on the Fly
I do, of course, realize the importance that birds play in our earth's ecosystem. Birds eat insects keeping their populations under control. They are a natural way to control pests in gardens, on farms, and other places. They also transport a variety of important items through the environment. They pollinate many flowering species of plants. Seeds that pass through the birds' digestive tracts fall to the ground and introduce plants into new areas. Birds are a vital food source to animals as well as humans. Predatory birds eat small mammals and fish, thus playing an important part in the world's natural food chain. Birds are critical to earth's cycle of life. Birds are also an excellent natural indicator of the health of many ecosystems.

Knowing all of that, I still have no doubt in my mind that God had a lot more on his mind than practicality when he created the over 10,000 different species of these winged delights that exist today. I am continually enthralled by their beauty, color, and unending variety of songs. Not all of that esthetic wonder would have been necessary just to sustain the earth. Rather, birds reveal the brilliant artistry of our Creator. In fact, like all the rest of his creation, as we observe and study birds, we come to discover they tell us as much about their Creator as the creatures themselves. In today's scriptures we read that "God created . . . every winged bird according to its kind. And God saw that it was good". Not just good from a pragmatic point of view, but good from the perspective of a Master Artist who built beauty and wonder into everything he made, for those willing to open their eyes and see. You might call that a bird's eye view.

Birder's Journal

2. A Creation Song

Morning Song: *And God blessed them, saying,
"Be fruitful and multiply and fill the waters
in the seas, and let birds multiply on the earth"
(Genesis 1:22)*

Winging Through the Word
Read: Psalm 104:1-24

Thoughts on the Fly
In the beginning there was no birdfeeder in our backyard,
and our backyard was void and without birds. My husband
said, "Let us get a birdfeeder" and arrived home one day with
an 8-foot shepherd's hook pole and a tubular-shaped finch
feeder. And behold, we suddenly had finches—lovely
yellow goldfinches and red house finches, filling the yard
with color and the melodious sound of birds. I'm not sure
why we decided to start with a finch feeder but I remember
being absolutely amazed that we could set up a birdfeeder
and within a few days have a nonstop flow of activity. But
what about all the other kinds of birds, I asked myself? It
wasn't long before there was a second pole, with more hooks,
and different kinds of feeders soon followed by a whole new

variety of winged delights. I quickly decided that one could never have quite enough birdfeeders.

While the first few chapters of Genesis are probably best known for being the Bible's Creation account, Psalm 104 is another more poetic version of the Creation story—a musical one. How appropriate to talk about the creation of birds in the form of a song. It describes how all of "the birds of the heavens" sing in the branches. Then it tells us that all of God's creatures "look to you, to give them their food in due season." It's almost as if the whole earth is the Lord's giant birdfeeder. And the Psalmist's response is to sing: "I will sing to the Lord as long as I live; I will sing praise to my God while I have being" (Ps 104:33). As a bird lover and a musician, I can only say that I'm pretty sure I need to get myself a few more birdfeeders.

Birder's Journal

3. What's in a Name?

Morning Song: *"Now out of the ground the Lord God had formed every beast of the field and every bird of the heavens and brought them to the man to see what he would call them. And whatever the man called every living creature, that was its name."*
(Genesis 2:19)

Winging Through the Word
Read: Genesis 2:1-20

Thoughts on the Fly
It is amazing to me that God, the Creator of the Universe and everything in it, would give the responsibility of naming his earthly creatures, including "every bird of the heavens" to humankind. I wonder what criteria he used to name them. I wonder what language they were first named in (probably the same one Adam spoke). I also wonder why God would give this responsibility to another one of his creatures. Though, I think the Bible gives us a pretty good idea. Of all that the Lord created, it was only humankind who he made in his own image. So, he knew we were designed to be creative. And being such a loving Heavenly Father to his newly created

children, it makes perfect sense that he would put us right to work doing something he knew we would love to do.

But I think God had another reason to give us the task of making sure each of his creatures had its own name. Names are extremely important to God. Not just bird names, but all names. Every one of us! There are over seven billion people in the world today (never mind all of the generations that have lived prior to today). God not only knows every single person who ever lived, by name, but he has called every single person, by name, to be his own beloved son or daughter. We are told, ". . . Fear not, for I have redeemed you; I have called you by name, you are mine" (Is. 43:10). But that's not even where it ends. He calls each of us by name, but ultimately he invites each of us to be called by his name. I wonder if Adam thought about that as he named all those birds.

Birder's Journal

4. New Beginnings

Morning Song: *"And the dove came back to him in the evening, and behold, in her mouth was a freshly plucked olive leaf. So Noah knew that the waters had subsided from the earth"* *(Genesis 8:11)*

Winging Through the Word
Read: Genesis 8:1-19

Thoughts on the Fly

Almost everyone knows the story. Noah built an ark. The animals (and birds) boarded it, two by two, and off they went riding high and dry above the flood that claimed the lives of every other living creature. It rained for 40 days but it would be another seven months before the giant floating zoo would finally settle itself on a mountaintop. It was 10 months before the water had receded enough for Noah to send out a raven to see if it would find dry land. Ravens are part of the crow family. These strong and acrobatic fliers are also effective hunters as well as scavengers that can live off of carrion or dead animals. So, it was probably not a big surprise that the raven never returned. Noah then sent out a dove. Doves and pigeons are in the Columbidae family. They live on seeds or fruit and are known for their ability to find their way home. Hence, after finding no place to land, the dove returned to the ark. A week later, Noah sent her out again. This time she returned with an olive branch. The following week, she did not return. The dove had found a new home—a new beginning—as would every living creature on the ark.

Sometimes God allows us to face some pretty difficult circumstances. Even though he doesn't always keep us from going through the storms, he has promised to go through them with us and carry us safely through. He assures us, "when you pass through the waters, I will be with you; and through the rivers, they shall not overwhelm you . . ." (Is 43:2). Sometimes, once the storm has passed, we find that he has taken us to a whole new place—a place of beautiful new beginnings.

Birder's Journal

5. Every Color of the Rainbow

Winging Through the Word
Genesis 9:1-17

Thoughts on the Fly

My dad (who loves watching birds as much as I do) got me a 365 Day Audubon bird calendar for Christmas. From arctic penguins to tropical toucans, every day of the year offers a different exquisitely beautiful and colorful picture of birds from all over the world. One could quickly reach the conclusion that the Creator loves color as one discovers that birds come in almost every color of the rainbow. For that matter, the God who created such magnificently colored birds (as well as flowers, tropical fish, and sunsets), is the one who created the rainbow. And he created the rainbow with all of its extravagant colors as a covenant—not just with humankind but with every living creature on the earth. God used his banner of color to remind us of his binding promise to his creation—to us.

Scientists have helped us understand that a rainbow is an optical phenomenon caused by the reflection of light in water droplets in the earth's atmosphere. The rainbow is a large band of parallel stripes that are actually a display of all of the colors that come from the Sun. White light contains all of the colors of the visible spectrum. When the light passes through a prism (the water droplets), it bends the light and spreads it into all of its colors. So, it is from the light of the Sun that all of the colors of the rainbow are created. It is from the Son— the Light of the world—that all of the colorful creatures in this lovely world were created. We are told, "all things have been created through him and for him . . . and in him all things hold together" (Col 1:16,17). And it is through the Son that his covenant will never be broken.

Birder's Journal

6. Appropriately Named

Morning Song: . . . *This is my name forever, and thus
I am to be remembered throughout all generations
(Exodus 3:15)*

Winging Through the Word
Read: Exodus 3:1-22

Thoughts on the Fly
I saw a flash of red streak through the sky and then saw a
bird I had never seen before at our camp feeder. It was a
rose-breasted grosbeak. Though the bird is fairly common in
the US, it is unique to North America. The name grosbeak
is derived from the French word "grosbec," meaning "big
beak." The broad and inclusive grosbeak family is made up
of several different species of distantly related songbirds.
Some grosbeaks such as the evening grosbeak or the pine
grosbeak are members of the finch family and clearly resem-
ble their smaller counterparts. The rose-breasted grosbeak
is actually in the cardinal family. It is a striking bird with its
black head, back, wings, and tail contrasting its bright white
under parts. It gets its name from its bright rosy red breast.
Despite their many differences, grosbeaks are uniformly

characterized by their large conical shaped bills. The species was definitely appropriately named no matter what language you say it in.

Names are very important to God, too. When he appeared to Moses in the wilderness and called him to lead his people out of captivity, Moses asked what he should tell them if they asked him for the name of his God, especially in a land where the people believed in many gods. The Lord uses different names throughout the Scriptures to identify himself and to reveal specific attributes of himself to his people (Adonai, Elohim, etc), but the name he gave to Moses was "I Am Who I Am" or the LORD. The Hebrew word for LORD is the divine name, YHWH, which is comes from the verb, "to be". God's name, the "I Am" reveals the fullness of his nature as the one true, ever-existent God. It is the name above all names.

Birder's Journal

7. Eagles' Wings

Morning Song: *"You yourselves have seen what I did to Egypt, and how I carried you on eagles' wings and brought you to myself"* *(Exodus 19:4)*

Winging Through the Word
Read: Exodus 14:16-31

Thoughts on the Fly

I had not heard the expression, "bucket list", but once it was explained to me, I realized that I've had a bucket list (things I want to do or see before I die) for most of my adult life. Topping the list—I wanted to see an eagle in the wild. I finally did. I was out kayaking when I spotted the nest at the top of a tree. As I stared in wonder at this amazing sight, I could see the shadows of two large baby eagles staring back out at me. I resisted the urge to shout for joy! The American Bald eagle is not actually bald. It is a large brown raptor with a white head and tail. It is considered to be one of the largest true raptors in North America. Ironically, in the late 20th century eagles almost went extinct in the US. Thanks to good wildlife management, the eagle has made a remarkable comeback and is no longer on the list of endangered species. It is becoming more common to see this majestic creature soaring through the sky with its wingspan of up to seven feet. More common but never any less awe-inspiring.

The Lord used the illustration of an eagle to describe how he rescued his people from their captors. Eagles are also known for their excellent vision, being able to spot prey over an area of almost 3 square miles from a fixed position. One of the Hebrew names of God is El Roi meaning "The God Who sees me" (Gen. 16:13). What an awe-inspiring picture that gives us of the God who hovers over his children and never lets them out of his sight. There is no safer place than under his protective wings and his watchful eye.

Birder's Journal

8. Nature's Cleanup Crew

Morning Song: *And these you shall detest among the birds; they shall not be eaten; they are detestable: the eagle, the bearded vulture, the black vulture (Leviticus 11:13)*

Winging Through the Word
Read: Leviticus 11:1-18

Thoughts on the Fly

It reminded me of a scene out of an old TV western. Not the Thousand Islands. I was kayaking by an island and was surprised to see a flock of buzzards converging in a small area. As I got closer I could see that they were dining on a dead carp that had washed ashore. Even though I was still feeling very much alive, I decided not to venture any closer. I later learned that the "buzzards" were actually Turkey Vultures. The next time I paddled by the island not even a bone was left. The Turkey Vulture gets its name from its similar appearance to a wild turkey with its featherless red and wrinkled head and neck, and dark body. It is over two feet tall with a wingspan of up to six feet. However, unlike the turkey, Turkey Vultures are masterful fliers and can be easily identified by their graceful soaring style. Despite their grace in flight, they are best known as scavengers that eat prey which is already dead. The Lord gave them a superior sense of smell enabling them to sniff out carrion from great distances. He has also given them a key role in being part of nature's cleanup crew.

As God's children traveled through the wilderness one of the ways he cared for them was to give them dietary rules and restrictions. They were forbidden to eat birds that were carnivores or scavengers. From this, we can see God's perfect plan for keeping his natural world clean and beautiful, and for keeping his people safe and healthy. But just as he cares for the upkeep of his natural world we who are made in his image are encouraged to do the same, and not leave it all to the Turkey Vultures.

Birder's Journal

9. The Eagle's Nest

Morning Song: . . . *like an eagle that stirs up its nest and hovers over its young, that spreads its wings to catch them and carries them aloft.* (Deuteronomy 32:11)

Winging Through the Word
Read: Deuteronomy 32:1-14

Thoughts on the Fly
When I spotted my first eagle's nest, I was thrilled. It was at the top of a tall pine tree on an island. I knew it was an eagle's nest because there were signs letting people (like me) know this was a protected area and to keep a distance. But the size of the nest alone would have told me what it was. The American Bald Eagle holds the record for the largest nest of any North American bird, and the largest tree nests of any bird in the world. Nests have been found that were over nine feet in diameter and weighing over two tons (I wonder how they weighed it). Part of the reason they get so big is because the eagle will return to the same nest each year and add to it so that it increases in size with each nesting season.

In this particular nest, I spotted two baby eagles looking back at me. I was about to ask myself where the mother bird was, but the thought was cut off by the shrill cry of a giant eagle soaring over the nest. She swooped down and dropped a large fish into the nest. The little ones lunged into action as the mother eagle landed on the branch above them. She majestically looked down at her hungry brood as they ate. Yet she was ever-vigilantly keeping her eye out for danger. The Lord used the image of an eagle to describe how he watches over each of his children. When we place ourselves under his loving care—under his wings—we can rest assured he will care for us. As the Psalmist put it, "You, Lord, will keep the needy safe and will protect us forever from the wicked" (Psalm 12:7).

Birder's Journal

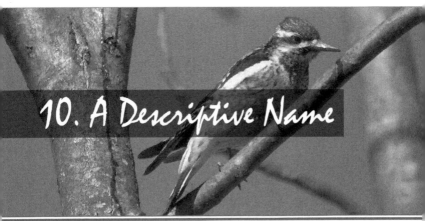

Photo courtesy Mike's Birds

Morning Song: *Then Gideon built an altar there to the Lord and named it The Lord is Peace (Judges 6:24)*

Winging Through the Word
Read: Judges 6: 7-24

Thoughts on the Fly
Many of the names given to different bird species are as much descriptions as they are names. Some birds were named by the sound they make. The Chipping Sparrow chips. The warbler warbles. The mockingbird "mocks" the sounds of other birds. And of course the cuckoo bird coo coos (they even named a clock after him). Other birds are named by how they look. A Red Winged Blackbird . . . (I don't think I need to explain that one). Bluebirds are blue, goldfinches are gold, blackbirds are black, and grosbeaks have big beaks. Other birds are named for what they do. Flycatchers catch flies, gnatcatchers catch gnats, berrypeckers peck berries, Honeyeaters eat honey, woodcreepers creep on wood, and woodpeckers peck on wood. All of life should be this easy to understand. My favorite bird name of all, the yellow-bellied

sapsucker is a combination of what he does and how he looks.

Since our God is so far beyond our limited human ability to comprehend, he has revealed many of his attributes to us through the different names he has to given us of himself. The first name of God found in the Scriptures is: "In the beginning, God (Elohim) created the heavens and the earth." Elohim is a plural word which points to the triune nature of the Creator and one true God. Other names for God include Adonai (Lord), El Elyon (God Most High), El Roi (God who sees) and El Shaddai (God Almighty). He is called YHWH Jireh (the LORD will provide), and YHWH Rapha (The LORD heals). What Gideon needed was God's peace so the name he revealed himself to Gideon as was YHWH Shalom (The LORD is peace). And the name that is above all names which meets every need we will ever have is Jesus.

Birder's Journal

11. A Love Story

Morning Song: *"May the Lord repay you for what you have done. May you be richly rewarded by the Lord, the God of Israel, under whose wings you have come to take refuge"*
(Ruth 2:12)

Winging Through the Word
Read: Ruth 2:1-20

Thoughts on the Fly

I was about to walk out our basement door when I saw a rapid motion and stopped in time to see a robin flying away. I soon discovered that the robin had built herself a nest, since the last time I went out the door, under the rafters of the deck. That was the last time my husband and I went out that door for the next month. Instead, we camped out by the basement window and watched as the mother bird laid her eggs, faithfully sat on her nest, and eventually cared for the four baby robins that hatched. Throughout some long days and very cold nights the mother robin never left the nest unless it was to lead any potential attackers (apparently like us) away. Other than that, she quietly and patiently sat with her wings spread over the four blue eggs keeping them warm and safe from predators.

The Book of Ruth is a love story. Actually, it is several love stories. It is the love story of a daughter-in-law who remained faithful to her husband's mother even after his death. It is a love story of how God would provide a new husband to love and care for young Ruth. Ultimately, the whole story is about a God who loves all of his children and faithfully provides for their needs. And the handsome prince in this particular love story reminded his future wife of the true hero of the story "under whose wings you have come to take refuge." Like the protective wings of the mother robin covering all of the eggs in her nest, the Lord was overseeing the love story of Ruth, Naomi, and Boaz. He is the same God of love who faithfully provides for each of his beloved children today.

Birder's Journal

12. God's Perspective

Morning Song: *For the Lord sees not as man sees: man looks on the outward appearance, but the Lord looks on the heart (1 Samuel 16:7)*

Winging Through the Word
Read: 1 Samuel 16:1-13

Thoughts on the Fly

There was no mistaking the sound. It was a gobble. And I could only think of one creature (other than a gobble-imitating hunter) that could make that kind of noise. Sure enough, as I quietly proceeded along the path, I spotted a wild male turkey who was undoubtedly strutting his stuff for the ladies. While they are best known for their gobble, turkeys have a number of different calls. The gobble is used by the males to let females know he is in the area. And he does it well. A wild turkey's gobble can be heard up to a mile away. Maybe that helps to make up for his looks. Not what I would consider the loveliest of creatures the males (or gobblers), in particular, have all kinds of appendages other fowl do not. In addition to their bristly breast beard, the gobblers have a fleshy growth called a wattle hanging beneath their chin. They have growths called caruncles on the side and back of the neck. The fleshy flap that hangs over the bill is called a snood (seriously). Yet, appearances aside, gobblers have keen eyesight, can fly up to 55 miles per hour, and can run up to 25 miles per hour. Plus, the females think they are really hot.

Benjamin Franklin actually thought the wild turkey was a proud looking creature and preferred it to the bald eagle for the national bird. I somehow can't picture the eagle being replaced by a wild turkey. Thankfully, God does not judge us humans by the same standards I have judged the turkey. God does not look at outside appearances; he looks at the heart. When he sees the heart of anyone sincerely trusting in him, He never sees a turkey. We are all eagles in his eyes.

Birder's Journal

_____

_____

_____

_____

_____

_____

_____

_____

_____

_____

_____

_____

_____

_____

13. The Explanation of Birds

Morning Song: *He spoke of trees, from the cedar that is in Lebanon to the hyssop that grows out of the wall. He spoke also of beasts, and of birds, and of reptiles, and of fish (1 Kings 4:33)*

Winging Through the Word
Read: 1 Kings 3:1-15

Thoughts on the Fly
It was a package deal and it included birds. Solomon had become the King of Israel after his father David died. Those were pretty big boots to fill, and Israel was a pretty big nation to lead. The Lord came to Solomon one night in a vision and told him to ask for anything he wanted. Rather than choosing riches for himself, Solomon asked for the wisdom needed to lead such a great nation. The Lord was pleased with that answer and not only gave Solomon the understanding he needed to be a king, but went above and beyond (as he always does), to make him the wisest man who ever lived. We are told that he spoke 3,000 proverbs and wrote 1,005 songs. He was also given knowledge about the natural world

including trees, plants, animals, and birds. People came from all over the world to hear him share his wisdom.

Today, knowledge about birds is called ornithology. Ornithology is the branch of the biological sciences that concerns the study of birds. The word "ornithology" comes from the ancient Greek words for bird (ornis) and explanation or rationale (logos). The science of ornithology has a long history that some claim goes as far back as Aristotle in 350 BC. I might point out that Solomon had him beat by hundreds of years. In one of his Proverbs Solomon wrote that "The fear of the Lord is the beginning of wisdom" (Prov. 9:10). The word "logos" also translates into the "Word". The Bible calls Jesus the Logos (John 1:1). God came in the flesh as the explanation of himself to humankind. When we put our trust in him he will give us a deeper understanding of himself that will go above and beyond our expectations (as he always does).

Birder's Journal

14. Meals on the Fly

Photo courtesy Harald Hoyer

Morning Song: *You shall drink from the brook, and I have commanded the ravens to feed you there (1 Kings 17:4)*

Winging Through the Word
Read: 1 Kings 17:1-16

Thoughts on the Fly

Ravens are one of the most mentioned birds in the Bible. It was the first living creature to be sent from Noah's ark after the flood. Jesus used the raven as an illustration of how God cares for his children. But my favorite reference to the raven is found in 1 Kings where the Lord used them to provide for his prophet Elijah. The Common Raven is an entirely black bird including its legs, eyes and beak. It is about two feet tall with a 46-inch wingspan. It can be identified by its large and thick bill with a curved tip. It has a large vocabulary of calls that include croaks, knocks, gurgles, whistles and screams. Ravens are acrobatic flyers that can perform swift turns, rolls, and can even fly upside down. They are carnivores so they can be spotted near highways looking for dead animals. Ravens are also considered to be among the smartest of all birds. Scientists have found that they can solve all kinds of extremely complicated problems and challenges.

Perhaps that is one reason God called upon the ravens to bring meals to Elijah day and night throughout the drought that ravaged the land. One can see from this that even when the Lord allows bad things to happen, in the world or even in our personal lives, he never stops providing for us. Jesus warned his disciples that there would be some difficult times ahead for them but he also assured them, "I have said these things to you, that in me you may have peace. In the world you will have tribulation. But take heart; I have overcome the world" (John 16:33). The God who created the world can use anything—even the ravens—to provide for us in our time of need.

Birder's Journal

15. The Eyes of the Lord

Photo courtesy Steve Wilde

Morning Song: *For the eyes of the Lord run to and fro throughout the whole earth, to give strong support to those whose heart is blameless toward him (2 Chronicles 16:9)*

Winging Through the Word
Read: Psalm 33:1-11

Thoughts on the Fly

The peacock is one of the most colorful and dramatically marked birds in the world. While most of us call them peacocks, that is only the correct name for the male. Females are called peahens, babies are called peachicks, and the whole group is called peafowl. Peafowl are the second largest member of the pheasant family. The males are known for their exotic iridescent tails also known as the fan or train that is more than half the length of the bird's body and is adorned with colorful "eye" markings of blue, gold, and red. All of that elaborate color has a practical purpose. The peacock's train is used to attract its mate. He arches it into a magnificent fan reaching across his back to the ground on either side. Peahens are believed to choose their mates according

29

to the quality of their suitor's feather trains. The peacock is the national bird of India. In the Hindu religion, it is a sacred bird, because the spots on the peacock's tail symbolize the eyes of their gods.

It is interesting that Hindus find significance in their gods' eyes. The Scriptures tell us that the Lord is always keeping a watchful eye out for each of his beloved children. We are told, "Behold, the eye of the Lord is on those . . . who hope in his steadfast love" (Psalm 33:18). Our God sees all of the world—all of eternity, for that matter—at a glance. He tells us, "I am God, and there is none like me, declaring the end from the beginning and from ancient times things not yet done" (Isaiah 6:9-10). He sees the story of our lives from beginning to end because he, himself, is "the first and the last, the beginning and the end" (Rev. 22:13).

Birder's Journal

_____

_____

_____

_____

_____

_____

_____

_____

_____

_____

_____

_____

_____

_____

_____

_____

_____

_____

16. The Birds Will Tell You

Photo by Heather Paul

Morning Song: *"But ask the beasts, and they will teach you; the birds of the heavens, and they will tell you"* *(Job 12:7)*

Winging Through the Word
Read: Job 12:1-13

Thoughts on the Fly

I was out working in the garden not far from our five bird feeders when I suddenly got buzzed. No, it had nothing to do with alcohol. And nothing to do with bees, though at first I thought a giant bee was coming after me. I looked up just in time to see a small hovercraft poised in midair looking directly into my face. I was being buzzed by a humming-bird. It was probably a combination of being in the flower garden and wearing a red shirt that had caught the curious little guy's attention but I suddenly realized that we needed to add a hummingbird feeder to our collection. As soon as we did, we had a steady stream of brilliantly iridescent ruby-throated hummingbirds join our steadily growing list of regular customers. The hummingbird is the smallest bird in the world. There are 325 hummingbird species in the world but only a few species reside in the US. The average ruby-throated hummingbird weighs 3 grams (just a little more than a penny). They are like miniature helicopters being the only birds that can hover mid-air as well as fly backwards, sideways, and even upside down. In fact, the little guy comes better equipped and with more maneuverability than any human-made aircraft.

The Book of Job is considered to be the oldest book in the Bible some dating Job, himself, to as far back as almost 2000 years BC (long before helicopters). But Job understood that when one looks at the intricate detail and marvelous design of even the tiniest creatures in the world, one must conclude that only the hand of a Master designer/technician/artist could have come up with such an amazing creature. As Job put it, "In his hand is the life of every creature".

Birder's Journal

17. Songs in the Night

Morning Song: . . . *Where is God my Maker, who gives songs in the night . . . makes us wiser than the birds of the heavens?* (Job 35:10-11)

Winging Through the Word
Read: Job 35:9 – 36:11

Thoughts on the Fly

We sat on the deck well past sunset just soaking in the wonder and beauty of the day's fading glow. As dusk set in, to our delight, we heard the sound of a loon giving its ethereal wail across the water. The call was answered by another loon in the distance. The two went back and forth for a while but then both broke into their antiphonal tremolos until the concert finally faded away into evening air. I realized I had been holding my breath to not miss a single moment. Without a doubt, the Common Loon is my favorite water fowl. It is a magnificent large black bird with white spots on its back. The loon has excellent diving skills and high speed flight, but is best known for its mystical calls heard over the water. Loons actually have four distinct calls: The hoot (a short, single note), the yodel (a territorial call given only by the male), the wail (their most common call), and the tremolo (which sounds like laughter).

Whenever I heard a loon call across the water I think of the words, "God my Maker who gives songs in the night". The loon sings its eerie songs through the darkest hours of the night. Young Elihu in the Book of Job chastises those who do not cry out to the God who "makes us wiser than the birds of the heavens" in their darkest hours. He explains that "God is mighty, and does not despise any" and that those who seek him will "complete their days in prosperity, and their years in pleasantness". I can't help thinking that God gave us the songs of the loon to remind us that we, too, can sing through our darkest hours knowing he will see us through to the dawn.

Birder's Journal

18. Made to Run

Photo courtesy "Son of Groucho"

Morning Song: *The wings of the ostrich flap joyfully, though they cannot compare with the wings and feathers of the stork (Job 39:13)*

Winging Through the Word
Read Job 39:1-18

Thoughts on the Fly

We don't have too many ostriches here in New York. Actually, other than the zoo, we don't have any. The ostrich is the world's largest bird. It is native to Africa and roams the African deserts getting most of its water from the plants it eats. The ostrich roams, in part, because despite having feathers and wings, it is flightless. But there is no need to feel sorry for the ostrich. Though they can't fly, ostriches were designed to be swift runners, sprinting up to 43 miles per hour. Their wings actually act as rudders to help them change direction while running. Their long legs can cover up to 15 feet in a single stride. Their two-toed foot has a long, sharp claw and they have a kick that can kill a predator as ferocious as a lion.

In the Lord's response to Job's questions about his suffering, God did not make any attempt either to explain or defend himself (after all, he is God). What he did do was point to his creation and what we can learn about him through the creatures he has made. He describes the ostrich and how it is no match in the air for the stork. One might question whether a flightless bird was a mistake. But he goes on to explain how she can outrun even the swiftest rider. There are no mistakes in God's creation. That should be of great encouragement to us. We tend to look at our own weaknesses and inabilities instead of focusing on the strengths God has given us. We may not be able to kick lions or outrun horses, but as long as we don't put our head in the sand, each of us has been uniquely designed to make a difference in this world.

Birder's Journal

_____

_____

_____

_____

_____

_____

_____

_____

_____

_____

_____

_____

_____

_____

_____

_____

_____

19. Let Us Prey

Photo courtesy Lisa Blystone

Morning Song: *"Does the hawk take flight by your wisdom and spread its wings toward the south?"*
(Job 39:26)

Winging Through the Word
Read Job 39:19-40:2

Thoughts on the Fly

I looked out the window and our feeders were filled with birds. When I looked again a few minutes later there were none. Our normally busy bird-filled backyard was totally abandoned. I glanced up at a nearby tree and quickly understood why the hasty retreat. There, staring down at the now empty scene was a large Red-tailed Hawk. The Red-tailed Hawk is the most common hawk in North America. It ranges from 18 to 26 inches tall with a wingspan from 45 to almost 60 inches. It is a bird of prey and can often be seen in tree branches or on utility poles hunting for mice, squirrels, rabbits, or other small animals. It is sometimes also referred to as a Chicken Hawk (the name Looney Tunes' Foghorn Leghorn used). As the name and Foghorn Leghorn imply, the Red-Tailed Hawk also preys on other birds. So, I have learned that when all of the birds disappear it is probably because they prefer to miss a meal rather than risk being one.

The Lord responded to Job by describing the hawk and the eagle and how they hunt prey for their young. He was not being insensitive to Job's suffering. After all, God himself was taking the time to respond to Job's questions. He was helping Job refocus from unanswered questions to a world of wonder and of order. The harsh reality of the animal kingdom is that animals eat other animals to survive. Life springs from death. That is a principle built into God's kingdom, and this was something Job clearly understood when he declared, "I know that my redeemer lives, and that in the end he will stand on the earth. And after my skin has been destroyed, yet in my flesh I will see God" (Job 19:25,26).

Birder's Journal

20. Raptors

Morning Song: *"I know that you can do all things, and that no purpose of yours can be thwarted"* *(Job 42:2)*

Winging Through the Word
Read Job 42:1-17

Thoughts on the Fly

Raptors are birds of prey that hunt live animals. The word raptor comes from the Latin word "rapere" meaning "to seize or plunder." Raptors are characterized by a hooked beak, powerful feet with sharp talons and keen eyesight. The raptor's beak has a curved tip with sharp cutting edges to tear apart its prey. Raptors also have powerful leg and toe muscles ending with sharp talons, making their feet lethal weapons. The raptor family has some incredible and almost mind-boggling abilities. A Red-tailed Hawk can spot a mouse from 100 feet. A Ferruginous Hawk is fierce enough to scare coyotes away from its nest. The American Kestrel can hover in the air while looking for small animals or insects. The Peregrine Falcon can dive at a speed up 200 mph. The Osprey can dive into the water talons first and completely submerge itself to catch its prey. The owl can hear a mouse step on a twig up to 75 feet away or can detect a lemming burrowing under the snow. The Barn Owl can hunt by sound only in the middle of the night.

The Book of Job ends with Job's response to the reply God gave him in regard to his seemingly meaningless suffering. God spoke of the many wonders of his creation and ended by describing the Behemoth and the Leviathan. Like raptors, they were both creatures of incredible and deadly strength. It was at this point that Job acknowledged "Surely I spoke of things I did not understand, things too wonderful for me to know" (Job 40:3). The God who created Leviathans, Behemoths, and raptors is infinitely more powerful than any of these works of his hands, and when we place our lives in those caring hands, we will be infinitely safe and secure.

Birder's Journal

21. Taming the Mighty

Photo by M. Bevis Photos

Morning Song: *You have given him dominion over the works of your hands . . . the birds of the heavens, and the fish of the sea . . . (Psalm 8:6-8)*

Winging Through the Word
Read Psalm 8:1-9

Thoughts on the Fly
While you really can't (and shouldn't) make a pet out of a wild raptor, for thousands of years, humankind has trained wild birds of prey to hunt for them. Falconry is the hunting of wild game by using a trained raptor. The sport was first developed almost four thousand years ago by the Chinese and Persians. During the Middle Ages falconry was brought to Europe, where it was called the sport of kings. In the US, falconry is highly regulated by the government. According to the US Fish and Wildlife Service, approximately 60% of all raptors used for falconry are Red-tailed Hawks with the American Kestrel being the second most popular. It is illegal to tame a raptor unless it is an imprint (a baby raptor raised by humans from birth). Unlike wild birds, imprints associate themselves with humans and are dependent on them until

they are adults. The adult raptor is then trained to hunt for the human. Since, in falconry, the raptor is always free to fly away and return to the wild, the human becomes dependent on the bird.

After we read about the unconquerable might of the Behemoth and Leviathan in the Book of Job, a few chapters later in the Psalms we are told that God has placed all of his creatures under the dominion of humankind. I am reminded of the Psalmist's words when I see how people can tame even the mighty raptors. Granted, many of the wild animals in the world today are dangerous and can harm or kill those who are not careful. But the day is coming when the "Son of Man" the Psalmist prophetically writes about will put all things under his feet and we, his children, will dwell with him and his creatures in perfect peace.

Birder's Journal

_____
_____
_____
_____
_____
_____
_____
_____
_____
_____
_____
_____
_____
_____
_____
_____
_____
_____
_____

Photo by William H. Majoros

Morning Song: *Even if my father and mother abandon me, the Lord will hold me close (Psalm 27:10 NLT)*

Winging Through the Word
Read Psalm 27:1-14

Thoughts on the Fly

It was the second time a robin built a nest under our deck. She laid her eggs and we waited excitedly for them to hatch. Actually, only one of the eggs hatched and the robin began caring for her chick. Then came the storm. A fierce wind blew throughout day and we could only hope that the nest was strong enough to withstand the gusts. To our dismay, the chick was blown out of the nest and was flailing helplessly on the ground below. To make matters worse, there was an overnight frost alert even though it was now late spring. We were horrified. We decided that the only chance the baby bird had would be if my husband put on gloves (to avoid human scent) and put the baby back in the nest. But when the mother bird returned, she flew down to the ground where the chick had landed, and seemed to not realize it was

43

now back in the nest. By the time she figured out what we had done, it was too late. The little bird did not survive the fall and the cold.

We humans, especially those of us who love birds, are heartbroken by the death of a tiny helpless bird. It is rare that human intervention can make a difference when a bird falls from the nest, and it is almost impossible that the bird would have survived on the ground. Psalm 27 is a beautiful reminder that we humans can never fall out of God's care. Even if friends and family fail us, we are never alone. And when the storms come, "he will hide me in his shelter in the day of trouble . . . he will lift me high upon a rock". He will see me safely through the storm.

Birder's Journal

_____
_____
_____
_____
_____
_____
_____
_____
_____
_____
_____
_____
_____
_____
_____
_____
_____
_____
_____

22. King of Fishers

Morning Song: *How precious is your steadfast love, O God! The children of mankind take refuge in the shadow of your wings (Psalm 36:7)*

Winging Through the Word
Read: Psalm 36:1-12

Thoughts on the Fly
I would have to humbly suggest that I have gotten pretty good at stalking wildlife. The one exception is the Kingfisher. They seem to almost always spot me first and are gone with their loud ratchety call before I even know they've been watching. That is probably because they spend most of their time perched on trees or other suitable high watchpoints close to water before plunging in head first after their fish prey. That's how they got their name as kings of the fisher birds. The Belted Kingfisher is the only kingfisher commonly found in the northern US and Canada. It is a medium-sized bird (about a foot) in length with a wingspan of 19 to 23 inches. It has a large blue head with a shaggy crest, a large white collar, a large blue band on the breast, and white under parts. It is one of the few bird species where the female is

more brightly colored than the male. Belted Kingfishers nest in a cavity at the end of a long tunnel they have excavated, usually in a riverbank of sand or clay. They have been known to share their tunnels with swallows. The swallows dig out small rooms tucked in the tunnel walls.

One has to wonder how the swallows know that, of all the predatory birds, the Belted Kingfishers will not only not harm them for encroaching on their nesting area, but that they will open their home to them. I think if I was a swallow, I would have a sense of security knowing I am sharing space with a bird as vigilant and protective as a kingfisher. The Psalmist shares a similar sense of security. He knows that the steadfast love of the King of kings will keep him eternally safe and secure.

Birder's Journal

24. Imago Dei

Morning Song: *By day the Lord commands his steadfast love, and at night his song is with me, a prayer to the God of my life (Psalm 42:8)*

Winging Through the Word
Read: Psalm 42:1-11

Thoughts on the Fly

When the loon concert began this time, we were ready for it. It was well after dark on a perfectly calm summer night. I had spotted several loons while out kayaking earlier that day so I was hoping they would stick around to serenade us tonight. As we sat on the porch, we listened to the pleasant sounds of crickets and tree frogs filling the evening air. We could hear the gentle cackling of nesting Great Blue Herons on the island across from our camp. Then, the star performers began. One loon wail was echoed by another, and then another each from further down the river. The closest voice then broke into a yodel, again answered from afar. Yet another loon soared overhead in the dark sky identified by a moving tremolo heading up the river, perhaps to join one of the others. The calls finally ended fading back into the steady rhythms of the crickets and frogs. It was a stellar performance.

As I sat there in the dark, awed by the evening concert I had just heard performed by God's wondrous creatures, I was reminded of the Psalms that speak of "songs in the night". I am pretty sure the Psalmist wasn't speaking about loons and crickets, but the Lord certainly created a world that is filled with beautiful and melodious night sounds. He also uniquely created humankind with the capacity to appreciate them. God gifted us with the ability to appreciate beauty and to experience wonder. We are also told that we are the only works of his hands that were created in his image or, in Latin, we were created "Imago Dei". The Creator of beauty made us uniquely able to appreciate what he created and to see and hear it for what it really is: Beautiful.

Birder's Journal

25. Peace in the Storm

Morning Song: *He says, "Be still, and know that I am God"*
(Psalm 46:10)

Winging Through the Word
Read: Psalm 46:1-11

Thoughts on the Fly

It was a very windy day. I looked out at the bird feeders and saw them wildly swinging back and forth, and I figured no self respecting bird would try to dine under such turbulent conditions. I was totally wrong. The woodpecker landed on suet that was thrashing back and forth, and began pecking at it as if it were perfectly still. The finches landed on the thistle feeder and began eating even though at times the feeder was nearly blowing horizontal. The sparrows arrived at the main feeder also violently swaying in the wind, and the chickadees touched down on the moving target just long enough to grab a sunflower seed and head to an equally moving branch to eat. It seems that the only one noticing that it was a windy day was me. All God's other creatures seemed perfectly content.

The Bible tells us we were made in the image of God. It also reveals God as a God of passion—love, wrath, joy, sorrow and a full range of the emotions we have been given. Great theologians have debated what it means to be Imago Dei. They have suggested three different ways we were made in God's imagine: Representative (having a nature, including our emotions, that is like God), Relational (our ability to have interpersonal relationships), and Functional (being like him in how we live). Since this is a book about birds, and not theology, I will leave any further explanation to the theologians. But getting back to that windy day, the Lord has told us to be still and know that our God will see us through our times of distress. He understands our emotions (he created them), but he offers peace even amidst the storms to those who seek refuge in him.

Birder's Journal

26. Headbangers

Morning Song: *I know all the birds of the hills,*
and all that moves in the field is mine
(Psalm 50:11)

Winging Through the Word
Read: Psalm 50:10-23

Thoughts on the Fly

We found that no backyard feeding station (or bird mall, as ours has become) is complete without a suet cage or two. As soon as we put one (or more) out, we had woodpeckers—all kinds of woodpeckers. They are some of our most faithful customers all four seasons of the year. There are over 180 species of woodpeckers worldwide and about 24 in the US. The most common species is the cute little downy woodpecker. Woodpeckers are probably best known for pecking wood. And they do it for all kinds of interesting reasons. They peck to get bugs from trees. But they also peck, or drum, to communicate with each other. They drum on trees, metal signs, utility poles and anything else that will make noise, to establish their territory. The males also drum to attract mates. One would imagine they must have frequent headaches from all that head banging. In reality, woodpeckers have reinforced skulls that are structured to handle the impact force, and their brains are well cushioned and protected. So, female woodpeckers can sit back and enjoy those drum solos with none of the concerns that go along with human headbangers. I do have to admit that a male woodpecker banging on a metal sign outside when I'm trying to concentrate has been known to give me a headache.

One could conclude that woodpeckers have been remarkably designed to do what they do best. One would then have to realize that such perfect design necessitates the hand of a highly skilled Designer. The Psalmist sings the praises of this Creator God and reminds us that if we cry out to him in our "day of trouble" he who made all the birds of the hills (and trees) can be relied upon to deliver us.

Birder's Journal

27. The Shadow of His Wings

Photo courtesy USFWS

Morning Song: *"Be gracious to me, O God, be gracious to me, for my soul takes refuge in Thee; and in the shadow of Thy wings I will take refuge, until destruction passes by" (Psalm 57:1)*

Winging Through the Word
Read: Psalm 57:1-11

Thoughts on the Fly

When I read Psalm 57, I can't help but to envision the wings of an eagle. Throughout the 35 days of incubation, the male and female eagles share the responsibility to insure that the eggs are continually covered so they are kept warm and protected from predators. Once the eaglets have hatched, the two adults are kept just as busy trying to satisfy their young ones' insatiable appetites. The eaglets will gain a pound every four or five days. By six weeks, they will be nearly as large as their parents. By eight weeks their appetites are at their greatest (compare them to human teenagers) forcing mom and dad to hunt almost continuously to keep them fed. It will be about 20 weeks before the young eagles are old enough to be on their own. Until then, neither parent goes more than a mile from the nest at any time. Their little ones will be safe under the shadow of their wings.

The Psalmist sings of finding safety under the shadow of the Lord's wings. Obviously, God does not have physical wings. But the illustration he gives us of himself helps us understand the kind of protective covering we always have when we place ourselves under his care. There's a big word for that, by the way. It is called "Anthropomorphism". As Theopedia explains, "The Bible has examples of God referring to himself in anthropomorphic terms . . . the purpose being to describe God in terms more understandable to humans. Without anthropomorphism, since God is invisible and immaterial, we would not have a framework on which to understand Him." I am so thankful for the picture God has given us of the refuge we find in him. Not just in our time of need, but every day of our lives.

Birder's Journal

28. Singing Through the Seasons

Morning Song: *for you have been my help, and in the shadow of your wings I will sing for joy (Psalm 63:7)*

Winging Through the Word
Read: Psalm 63:1-11

Thoughts on the Fly

My husband calls it the "me me" bird because of its hairdo that reminds him of Alfalfa from the Little Rascals. As long as we keep the menu to their liking, the Tufted Titmice are year-round regulars at our feeder. The Tufted Titmouse is a small, gray songbird, easily recognized for its tall crest (or "me me hairdo") of gray feathers on its head, its big black eyes, black forehead, and rust-colored flanks. They are fun to watch at the feeder as they open seeds by holding them in their feet and hammering them with their bill. Most Tufted Titmice live their entire life within a few miles of where they were born. Hence, they are year-round residents wherever they are found. They only live in areas where rainfall is greater than 24 inches per year, and are more common where rainfall exceeds 32 inches per year. The titmouse is sometimes called the "sugar bird" because it often sings in the winter when the sap in the maple trees begins to run.

It is nice to have birds that serenade us even through the winter months. While most of the other songbirds remain silent until spring, the "Sugar Birds" are a reminder that even though we do not yet see any change in the weather, better days are just ahead. For those of us who lean on the Lord we too have every reason to sing even through our seasons of darkness. We have the assurance that better days will come and that even in those difficult times, we can find comfort under the shadow of his wings. We may not be labeled as sugar birds, but hopefully the song of a sweet spirit will bring delight to him and draw others to the source of our joy.

Birder's Journal

29. The Night Songstress

Morning Song: *I said, "Let me remember my song in the night; let me meditate in my heart"*
(Psalm 77:6)

Winging Through the Word
Read: Acts 16:16-34

Thoughts on the Fly

Someone from Massachusetts who lived on Nightingale Pond Road asked on an online birding forum why, with a name like that, they had never spotted a single nightingale.

A reader posted a rather long response describing a guaranteed way to see nightingales. It ultimately involved a drive to the airport and a trip to the UK. There are no known nightingales living in the wild, here in the US. The term "Nightingale" actually means "night songstress". It is a small bird that is native to Europe and southwest Asia. Nightingales were named over 1000 years ago. They were so named because, unlike most birds, they sing at night as well as during the day. But it is only the males who do the evening serenades and, as one might suspect, they do so to attract females. They will continue singing into the morning hours and actually sing even louder, especially in urban settings, to make up for the extra background noise of an awaking city.

I love the thought of being a "night songstress". God gives us his song in the night, but it is when we sing our own songs—songs of praise—back to him that he turns even our darkest hours into light. When the Apostle Paul and Silas were beaten and thrown into prison, they had their own private praise concert around midnight and it quite literally rocked the house. The Lord caused an earthquake that set them free and the guard and his whole family came to believe in the God who Paul and Silas worshiped. Singing songs in the night—worshiping in our times of distress—brings glory to God, lifts our focus off of our trials, and also points others to the one who can give them something to sing about, too.

Birder's Journal

30. Fit for a King

Photo by Andy Morffew

Morning Song: *Even the sparrow finds a home,
and the swallow a nest for herself, where
she may lay her young, at your altars,
O Lord of hosts, my King and my God
(Psalm 84:3)*

Winging Through the Word
Read: Psalm 84:1-12

Thoughts on the Fly
There is a castle in the Thousand Islands that can be rented
(the whole castle) for the night. Singer Castle has a royal suite
that is truly fit for a king. We recently heard that there some
usurpers, however, who have been staying there for free. An
osprey couple decided to make themselves King and Queen
of the castle roof for the season. The osprey, also known as
the fish hawk, is a large raptor up to 25 inches tall with up to
a six foot wingspan. It is brownish black on its upper parts
and white below. It has a white head with a black eye patch.
Ospreys live almost exclusively on fish and are the only raptors that hunt by diving below the water's surface for their
prey. Their giant claws help them pluck fish from the water
and carry them for great distances with the fish pointing

headfirst to ease wind resistance. Hence, ospreys build their nests near the water on such varied sites as tree tops, buoys, electric towers, and even on occasion, castle roofs.

Birds have apparently had good taste in nesting locales since as far back as in the days of the glorious Temple in Jerusalem where "the swallow builds her nest." While most of us humans don't have the luxury of living in a castle or a temple, we do all have an open invitation to a far more glorious destination. God has invited each of us to be his personal guests in his eternal kingdom. We are told, "There is more than enough room in my Father's home . . . I am going to prepare a place for you" (John 14:2-3). Just think! We will be the sons and daughters of the King. Not for the night, but for eternity.

Birder's Journal

_____

_____

_____

_____

_____

_____

_____

_____

_____

_____

_____

_____

_____

_____

_____

_____

_____

_____

_____

31. Life Expectancy

Morning Song: *He will cover you with his pinions, and under his wings you will find refuge; his faithfulness is a shield and buckler (Psalm 91:4)*

Winging Through the Word
Read: Psalm 91:1-16

Thoughts on the Fly

I never really thought about it until we started making friends with chickadees. For the past several years when we arrive at our summer camp the chickadees are waiting for us, ready to land on our hands and be fed. That's when I started wondering how long birds live in the wild. I was surprised to learn that all of that fresh air and country living apparently serves them well. For example, I discovered that chickadees, wrens and hummingbirds can live up to nine years, bluebirds, warblers, orioles and downy woodpeckers can live up to 11 years, sparrows up to 15, and mourning doves have been documented up to 31 years. Several other factors were cited in how long different species live. Communal nesting helps extend life. The longer birds stay in a family group, the longer life expectancy they have. Migrating birds tend to live longer than those that don't. And in general, birds that live by the sea have the longest documented life expectancies with the Laysan albatross topping the list at up to 42 years.

There are several take-home points for us humans in the factors that determine long life for birds. First, it's a good excuse to live by the water. More importantly, we humans were not made to live alone or in isolation. The Bible tells us that "it is not good for man to live alone," to "not forsake assembling ourselves together" and by reminding us that in God's family every member is important. But the best secret to long life is found in our relationship with him. He has promised all who take refuge under his protective wings that "With long life I will satisfy him and show him my salvation." (Psalm 91:16). That gives us a life expectancy of forever.

Birder's Journal

32. A Song for All Seasons

Morning Song: *Oh sing to the Lord a new song;*
sing to the Lord, all the earth!
(Psalm 96:1)

Winging Through the Word
Read: Psalm 96:1-13

Thoughts on the Fly

They had been quiet throughout the cold winter months
but one day in early March I heard the first notes of a very
familiar song. The cardinals had started to sing again. There
was no doubt about it now—spring was on the way. Plenty
of other birds start singing in the spring or, more specifically,
as mating season approaches but there are several aspects
of the cardinals' songs that are unlike almost all other songbirds. Cardinals are unique in that both the male and female
birds sing. The cardinal's song is a loud string of clear down-
slurred or two-parted whistles, often ending in a slow trill.
When they aren't singing, cardinals have at least 16 different
calls, the most common being a loud warning chip. Though
males have been known to sing throughout the year, spring
and early summer is when the songsters reach their peak.
The female normally sings longer and in a more complex

melody and unlike other bird species, she will sing from her nest possibly to alert the male that she is in need of food. Perhaps in that regard, she's not all that different from us human females who are known on occasion for our complex conversations (we talk a lot).

The Lord encourages his children to sing songs of praise. Not just in our joyful seasons, but also in our times of wintry sorrow. He knows that when we take our focus off of our difficulties and look, instead, upon his glory, strength, and salvation, we are set free from the doubts and discouragement that can drag us down. Psalm 96 is a reminder to us that one day all of the earth will break out in a song of praise when the Lord returns as promised to make all things right.

Birder's Journal

_____

_____

_____

_____

_____

_____

_____

_____

_____

_____

_____

_____

_____

_____

_____

_____

33. A Bird in the Hand

Morning Song: *The birds of the sky nest by the waters; they sing among the branches (Psalm 104:12)*

Winging Through the Word
Read: Psalm 104:1-23

Thoughts on the Fly

I filled the palm of my hand with black sunflower seeds and stood out in the yard by the birdfeeder. The chickadees were obviously fascinated and curious. In fact, several of them started communicating with each other in little peep-like sounds. I was obviously the topic of conversation. One eventually moved to a branch that was fairly near my hand for a closer look. We stared at each other in silence for a while but he suddenly scolded me with the familiar "chick-a-dee-dee-dee" call they are known for and named after. I tried to assure him I meant no hard. He looked skeptical. I would be lying if I said it was quick and easy, but eventually, that feisty little chickadee landed on my hand just long enough to snatch a seed and fly off to a nearby tree to eat his little treat. He was back in a few minutes for another, and it wasn't long before several of his little friends decided to get in on the action. Today, I can walk out in the yard, hold out my hand with some seeds, and the not-so-wild chickadees come flocking to me for their (literal) hand-outs.

The Black Capped Chickadee is known to be a very outgoing and social little bird. When I stand with my hand out watching the little chickadees boldly land and grab their seeds, I am reminded of the Psalmist's words: "All creatures look to you to give them their food at the proper time . . . when you open your hand, they are satisfied with good things" (Psalm 104:28-29). I think it is delightful that the Creator allowed us to experience a tiny bit of the joy it must give him to care for our needs with his hand ever out-stretched toward us in love.

Birder's Journal

34. Food from God

Photo by Michael "Mike" L. Baird

Morning Song: *In them the birds build their nests; the stork has her home in the fir trees (Psalm 104:17)*

Winging Through the Word
Read Psalm 104:24-35

Thoughts on the Fly
It sounds like a jungle. Though the Thousand Islands is located in the northern-most part of the US, when we listen to the Great Blue Herons nesting on the island across from our camp on a hot summer night, it really sounds like a scene from a Tarzan movie. The Great Blue Heron is the largest heron in North America standing up to four feet tall with a wingspan of almost six feet. As its name indicates it is blue-gray in color with a plume of feathers on its chest and back. When they soar majestically overhead with their distinctive tucked-in neck and long legs trailing behind them, they remind me of a prehistoric pterodactyl (not that I've actually ever seen one). Herons are members of the long-legged wader family of stork-like birds. They are social birds, nesting in colonies in the tops of tall evergreen trees. When

they aren't in their treetop nests caring for their young, they are often seen standing motionlessly in shallow water hunting for fish. Once it spots its prey, the heron will spring into action and strike like lightning to grab a fish with a single thrust of its sharp bill. Then, with a loud squawk, it will leap into the sky and head back to a nest of hungry chicks awaiting breakfast.

The Great Blue Heron is an amazing sight whether it is fishing in the water or cackling in its treetop nest. The Psalmist writes about nesting birds and storks in his creation song. He, too, must have watched in wonder as they hunted for food to provide for their young. He concluded that all of these creatures were "seeking their food from God" and that even the prey they return to their nests with was created and provided by him.

Birder's Journal

35. Living Water

Morning Song: *He provides food for those who fear him; he remembers his covenant forever (Psalm 111:5)*

Winging Through the Word
Read: Psalm 111:1-10

Thoughts on the Fly

We realized that no bird lover's backyard is complete without at least one birdbath. We have one at home and at camp. When we were choosing our birdbaths, we discovered that the creative possibilities were virtually endless. In addition to the standard ceramic basin on a pedestal, birdbaths can be hung on chains or secured to poles or trees. They also come in durable polymer, lightweight resin or glass. They can be enhanced with heating elements to keep the water from freezing, or have battery-operated ripple effects to keep it fresh, or include a spraying fountain to attract birds. We picked one that had a planter on the bottom, a bird feeding platform over the bath, and a solar light at the top. I think we enjoy that colorful display almost as much as the birds that bathe in it.

What amazes me the most about birdbaths is that birds actually use them. And what is even more puzzling to me is that both our camp and our home are located right next to a large body of water. Why one would settle for a small ceramic container when one has the whole St. Lawrence Seaway to bathe in, is a bit of an enigma to me. It reminds me a bit of God's warning when his people stopped trusting in him. He said, "My people have committed two sins: They have forsaken me, the spring of living water, and have dug their own cisterns, broken cisterns that cannot hold water" (Jer. 2:13). It would be like drinking out of a dirty birdbath when the open waters of the river are available to you. As the Psalmist writes, we need to look no further than to our Creator to provide for all of our needs. I'll drink to that.

Birder's Journal

_____

_____

_____

_____

_____

_____

_____

_____

_____

_____

_____

_____

_____

_____

_____

_____

_____

36. You are What you Eat

Photo by Dimitry B.

Morning Song: *How sweet are your words to my taste, sweeter than honey to my mouth!*
(Psalm 119:103)

Winging Through the Word
Read: Psalm 119:1-16

Thoughts on the Fly
No, Pink Flamingos are not native to New York. Nevertheless, they have been known to make quite a few appearances in the area. The large plastic lawn ornaments can be spotted anywhere from inner city homes to rural campsites. The popular plastic pink birds were invented by Don Featherstone in 1957. And if one is feeling a little prankish, one can always "Pink Flamingo" someone's yard when they aren't looking (the more, the better). Real pink flamingos are tall wading birds that live in tropical climates. The word "flamingo" comes from the Spanish and Latin word "flamenco" which means fire, referring to the bright color of the birds' feathers. The chicks are born gray or white and take up to three years to reach their mature color. What some don't realize about the flamingo is that their bright color is due primary to their diet. The pink, orange or red color of a flamingo's feathers is

caused by carotenoid pigments that come from the shrimp, plankton, and crustaceans they eat. If they don't eat these foods, their feather color blanches to a dull white.

In much the same way that flamingos' colors are determined by their diet, the same could be said for us. If we want to live godly lives that glorify the Lord, we need to consume the kind of nutrition that brings those colors out in us. We are told to feast on the pure milk of the Scriptures. The Psalmist wrote, "I have stored up your word in my heart, that I might not sin against you". He understood that we really are what we eat. When we feed our minds and hearts with his Word, we will be able to show his true colors to the world and will be living in the pink.

Birder's Journal

37. The Early Bird

Morning Song: *I rise before dawn and cry for help; I hope in your words (Psalm 119:147)*

Winging Through the Word
Read: Psalm 119:137-151

Thoughts on the Fly

I consider them the first sign that spring is on the way. Sometimes the first sighting comes while snow is still on the ground. But as soon I see my first robin bobbin' across the backyard, I know it won't be too much longer until all of the other wonderful signs of spring will follow. The American Robin with its bright red breast, and distinctively complex song that is often heard before sunrise, is a migratory song-bird that is a member of the thrust family. Robins are abundant throughout North America, wintering in Florida and Mexico. When I think of the early bird catching the worm, it is the robin that comes to mind since we continually see them expertly pulling earthworms from the lawn. Robins aren't just the first to arrive back in the spring. They are the earliest birds to lay their eggs. You might call the robin the consummate early bird.

There's a lot to be said for being early (some of which I wouldn't personally be able to comment on, since I am definitely not a morning person). But the author of Psalm 119 is a self-identified early bird rising before the sun is even up to bring his requests to the Lord. He knew without a doubt that the Lord not only hears but responds to our cries for help. He wrote, "In my distress I called to the Lord, and he answered me" (Ps. 120:1). The Lord has declared, "When he calls to me, I will answer him; I will be with him in trouble; I will rescue him and honor him" (Ps. 91:15). That would give one a very good reason for getting up early. And for singing, too!

Birder's Journal

Photo by John Schell

Morning Song: *O Lord, you have searched me and known me! . . . you discern my thoughts from afar (Psalm 139:1)*

Winging Through the Word
Read: Psalm 139:1-24

Thoughts on the Fly

I have to admit that I never really liked them very much. I'm not sure why. They are actually very attractive large black birds. But it was my mother-in-law, Jessie, who helped me gain some appreciation for crows. She had befriended some of them to the point where they would see her through the window and call for her. She would then come to the door and throw them slices of bread. They were at her feet before the first piece hit the ground. Still, it wasn't until we arrived at camp and discovered a nest at the top of one of our own trees that we came to see crows in a whole new light. We watched as the parents diligently cared for their little ones until they left the nest. The crow family stayed close together for the rest of the summer. The American Crow is one of the most intelligent of all birds. I read that crows can recognize individual people, can even pick them out of a crowd and remember them for years. Conversely, people, even those who love crows, usually can't tell crows apart. That is called the Crow Paradox.

Some might claim there is a similar paradox between God and humankind. But there does not need to be. Our Creator desires to know and be known by every one of us. Intimately. Before we were even born he knew every detail of our life. But after singing of God's intimate knowledge, the Psalmist goes on to proclaim, "I praise you, for I am fearfully and wonderfully made. Wonderful are your works; my soul knows it very well". There is no paradox here. He shares a mutual love relationship with his Lord—the same relationship God wants to have with everyone. With you.

Birder's Journal

39. Complex Praises

Morning Song: *The eyes of all look to you, and you give them their food at the proper time. You open your hand and satisfy the desires of every living thing (Psalm 145:15,16)*

Winging Through the Word
Read: Psalm 145:1-21

Thoughts on the Fly

I love to feed our little chickadee friends from my hand, and I am pretty sure the feelings are mutual. I was out in the yard one day and was ill prepared when the first aerial flyby took place. I was about to head inside to get some seeds but suddenly realized, not to be deterred by a missing palm, the chickadee landed right on top of my cap and did his little chick-a-dee-dee scold to let me know he was dissatisfied with the service. I quickly returned with seeds and watched as he landed and immediately darted off with his prize. I learned not to take it personal that chickadees grab their food and fly somewhere else to eat it. Watching how they crack those seeds open on a tree branch with their beaks actually makes me grateful that they don't try to do it on my hand. From his tree branch I heard the little bird begin to make a variety of little peeps and chirps. He was apparently calling in reinforcements because moments later, a whole crew of chickadees arrived looking for treats.

In addition to the call they are named after, chickadees are known to have numerous other different vocalizations. Experts have classified 13 distinct types of calls, many of which are complex and are used to communicate different types of information. Obviously one is for inviting others to join them for a free meal. Psalm 145 is another song that speaks of the hand of God providing for all of his creatures. But it also describes how all of God's creatures give praise to him. The Psalmist doesn't specify how each creature does this, but it seems to me that all of the chickadees' highly complex calls sing the praises of their Master Designer.

Birder's Journal

40. One Good Tern

Morning Song: *He gives to the beasts their food, and to the young ravens that cry. (Psalm 147:9)*

Winging Through the Word
Read: Psalm 147:1-11

Thoughts on the Fly

I was kayaking in the middle of the shipping lane when I heard the sound of birds—many birds. I saw a channel marker with hundreds of terns flying around it. I later learned that volunteers built tern houses on several channel markers to help this currently "threatened" species make a comeback in New York State. Terns are graceful water fowl that are closely related to seagulls. The "Common Tern" is a medium-sized white or gray bird with a black cap, white wings with dark tips, and a long forked tail. They are aerial fish feeders and are often seen plunging into the water after their prey. They make harsh, single-note calls, which sound all the harsher when they are being disturbed on their nests by a kayaker. Judging from the number of birds I saw nesting on that particular channel marker, I would have to guess that the campaign has been a success so far. They seem to have created a whole tern-key operation out there.

It is exciting to know that we can truly make a difference in the protection and preservation of some of the endangered species on our planet today. When we do, we are following the example the Lord himself gave us in caring for his creation. We see how he has looked after each of his creatures through all of the provisions he made for them on this exquisitely designed planet. It is reassuring to know that he has promised to provide for our needs as well. We are told that "this same God who takes care of me will supply all your needs from his glorious riches, which have been given to us in Christ Jesus" (Phil 4:19). In his care, your life will definitely take a "tern" for the best!

Birder's Journal

_____

_____

_____

_____

_____

_____

_____

_____

_____

_____

_____

_____

_____

_____

_____

_____

_____

41. Murmurations

Morning Song: *Praise the Lord from the earth . . . Beasts and all livestock, creeping things and flying birds!*
(Psalm 148:7,10)

Winging Through the Word
Read: Psalm 148:1-14

Thoughts on the Fly

I saw it once in our own backyard and was amazed. Then I saw it again on a video that went viral a few years ago on YouTube*. It was simply breathtaking. I heard a sound one day and looked outside to see literally thousands of starlings covering our lawn. But as soon as they spotted me, they took off en masse and began soaring through the sky in patterns reminiscent of a highly choreographed dance. I later learned that there is a name for this glorious bird ballet. It is called a murmuration. The starling is a medium sized bird with glossy black plumage which is speckled some times of year. In flight their wings are short and pointed, making them look like small, four-pointed stars (hence, their name). Because he mentioned them in his writings, starlings were first brought to the US in the 19th century by Shakespeare enthusiasts.

Today, they are among our most numerous songbirds (some would say too numerous). They roost communally in flocks that may contain up to a million birds.

But when they come together in flight, the effect is absolutely stunning. Murmurations dazzle the fortunate onlookers with their extremely synchronized maneuvers, which seem to occur spontaneously. Scientists have studied starlings in an attempt to understand the how and why of murmurations. They can only theorize about the "why" but have discovered that the "how" involves something similar to cutting edge physics. Since most birds have very little formal education in physics, one could conclude that they must have an awesome Choreographer. In his song of praise to the Lord, the psalmist invites every living creature to take part in the performance. When I see something as awe-inspiring as a murmuration, I can't help but to join in the praises, too.

* Murmuration (Official Video) by Sophie Windsor Clive & Liberty Smith - https://www.youtube.com/watch?v=iRNqhi2ka9k

Birder's Journal

42. Crimson and Snow

Morning Song: *Come now, let us reason together, says the Lord: though your sins are like scarlet, they shall be as white as snow; though they are red like crimson, they shall become like wool (Isaiah 1:18)*

Winging Through the Word
Read: Isaiah 1:1-19

Thoughts on the Fly
It reminded us of our own backyard Christmas card. Our giant cedar tree was dotted with dollops of snow and sitting on one of the branches was a brilliant red cardinal. Actually, we think of him as *our* brilliant red cardinal. He and the Mrs. have been hanging out in our neighborhood ever since we started carrying black sunflower seeds as a staple in our feeder. Cardinals, which are also appropriately referred to as "redbirds," are so well loved that they have been named the official bird of seven U.S. states. They are year round favorites to many of us bird lovers since they do not migrate in the winter. They were traditionally more common in warmer climates in the south, but have expanded their range even as far as Canada. Some suggest this is possibly due to the

increased number of winter birdfeeders (including ours). The male Cardinal is one of the most recognizable and popular backyard birds because of its brilliant red color, crested head and black mask. The female cardinal is brownish gray in color. Both have red beaks. Not surprisingly, the cardinal was named by the early settlers after the Cardinals of the Catholic Church who wore red robes and hats.

Getting back to that Christmas card scene in our backyard, the Bible gives us a similar picture of red and white in the Book of Isaiah. The Lord speaks of washing away the blood-red sins of his rebellious people so that they can "become like wool". And he did this through the birth of his Son who would one day shed his own blood so that all who believe in him can be counted as white as snow. Christ's birth was only the beginning of a Christmas story that will carry us through eternity.

Birder's Journal

_____
_____
_____
_____
_____
_____
_____
_____
_____
_____
_____
_____
_____
_____
_____
_____
_____

43. Angry Birds

Photo by Don DeBold

Morning Song: *The Lord of Heaven's Armies will hover over Jerusalem and protect it like a bird protecting its nest . . .*
(Isaiah 31:5 NIV)

Winging Through the Word
Read Isaiah 31:1-9

Thoughts on the Fly

Possibly not every bird lover is a fan of the video game that has captivated much of the world, even if the superstars of the game are birds. *Angry Birds* was first released in 2009. Since then, over a billion people have downloaded the Angry Birds app making it the largest mobile app success in the world. Players use a slingshot to launch multi-colored cartoon birds at pigs hiding in various structures in an attempt to destroy all the pigs on the playing field. The pigs (in case you are wondering) have stolen the birds' eggs (now you know why the birds are angry). There are several different birds used in the game. In the beginning only Red Bird is available. As the player advances, additional birds with special abilities appear. Blue Bird can separate into three birds, Black Bird explodes, and White Bird can drop explosive eggs.

That may all sound a little harsh, but anyone who loves birds knows that a mother bird will do just about anything to protect her eggs. We have seen mother robins willing to risk their own lives to lead predators away from their nesting chicks. During nesting season, it is a common sight to see a large raptor being chased across the sky by a smaller bird, or bird couple defending their nest. I've been awed at not only the tenacity of the smaller birds, but also the efficacy at driving the predator birds out of the area. Even the angriest of birds would be no match for one of those little nesting momma birds. Clearly, God has hardwired his creatures to do whatever it takes to keep their young safe from impending danger. That is no doubt why the Lord repeatedly uses the illustration of a bird protecting its nest in describing the kind of care each of his children have under the shadow of his wings.

Birder's Journal

44. Giving A Hoot

Morning Song: *There the owl nests and lays and hatches and gathers her young in her shadow; indeed, there the hawks are gathered, each one with her mate (Isaiah 34:15)*

Winging Through the Word
Read: Isaiah 34:8-17

Thoughts on the Fly

I never got a glimpse of him, but I know he was out there. I woke up in the middle of the night to the familiar sound of an owl outside our window. I jumped out of bed and ran to turn on the floodlights but never spotted him. Owls are a group of birds best known for their distinct calls and their nocturnal lifestyle. They are predators and are excellent night hunters partly because they also have the ability to fly silently. Many species of owls have special flight feathers adapted to make them almost inaudible in flight. Another interesting feature owls have is that their eyes are fixed in their sockets so they need to turn their entire head to see in a different direction. However, they do have well-developed binocular vision. Owls are known for their trademark hoot but make a wide variety of vocalizations. The hoot is their territorial declaration (though not all owl species are able to hoot). They also make screeches, hisses and screams. I'm glad I wasn't woken up by one of those.

Isaiah 34 speaks of the day of the Lord's vengeance against his enemies—against those who have attacked or persecuted his people. Isaiah describes the wilderness that would be left once the Lord has brought judgment on the evil-doers. The land will be become inhabited by wild animals including the owl and her young. He goes on to say that "Not one of these shall be missing; none shall be without her mate". So even in the aftermath of God's punishment of evil humankind, he will still care for his animal kingdom and provide for them. Thankfully for us Isaiah went on in the next chapter to let us know what he has planned for those who trust in him.

Birder's Journal

45. Sanctuary

Morning Song: *the burning sand shall become
a pool, and the thirsty ground springs of water;
in the haunt of jackals, where they lie down,
the grass shall become reeds and rushes.
(Isaiah 35:7)*

Winging Through the Word
Read: Isaiah 35:1-10

Thoughts on the Fly

Sometimes when I feel like getting away from it all, even
getting away from the other boats and people out on the
water, I will kayak into a small bay behind our camp. Lily
bay is almost completely hidden from the rest of the boating
traffic—from the rest of the world, for that matter. It is a
private little world all its own that I can have all to myself.
Well, not exactly. The moment I paddle into the bay, in the
shallow waters surrounded by bulrushes, I find myself being
anything but alone. It is a secluded piece of the world that
is teeming with wildlife including ducks, herons, terns and
ospreys, as well as a chorus of songbirds, and red-winged
blackbirds. Sometimes a loon will even swim into Lily Bay

probably to escape all of the same river commotion that I do. It is a lovely and peaceful little bird sanctuary and none of them seem to mind sharing it with me one bit.

Isaiah wrote about the wilderness that would follow God's judgment upon the evil of this world. But he does not leave it there. In Isaiah 35, he goes on to describe the restoration that will follow. The dessert will bloom, the sand will become a stream filled with bulrushes and the world will be filled with creatures all living peacefully together in one big sanctuary. But best of all, the Lord himself will come to his beautiful and peaceful new sanctuary where no evil will ever be allowed again. And he will allow all of his people to enter in—a chorus of joyful worshipers—to this lovely and eternal dwelling. In the mean time, you can find me and all of my bird friends awaiting his return in Lily Bay.

Birder's Journal

_____

_____

_____

_____

_____

_____

_____

_____

_____

_____

_____

_____

_____

_____

_____

_____

_____

46. Mourning to Dancing

Photo by John Beetham

Morning Song: *I cried like a swift or thrush,*
I moaned like a mourning dove. My eyes
grew weak as I looked to the heavens.
I am being threatened; Lord, come to my aid!
(Isaiah 38:14 NIV)

Winging Through the Word
Read: Isaiah 38:1-20

Thoughts on the Fly
When I was a child, I always thought of it as a soft and com-
forting sound—a gentle coo that we often heard outside the
window in the morning. So it was only natural I would think
it was called a Morning Dove. At some point I realized that
the Mourning Dove got its name not for the hour of day, but
rather for a sound that some consider a cry of lament. The
other sound they are well known for is the whistling sound
they make as they take off and in flight. The Mourning Dove
is a graceful and small-headed dove with a soft gray-brown
body, black dots on its wings and a single black spot behind
and below its eyes. It has a long and slender tail with a white
edge. They frequently feed on the ground below our feeders, often in pairs. As for that sorrowful sound it makes, in

reality, the Mourning Dove's coo is its way of signaling the beginning of nesting season, attracting makes, claiming territory and raising its young.

King Hezekiah compared his own cries of sorrow to that of a Mourning Dove in the song he wrote to the Lord. But his song was no more a song of lament than that of the Mourning Dove. The Lord had heard Hezekiah's prayer and had healed him from a fatal illness. Now, Hezekiah was singing a song of Joy. The Psalmist, too, wrote about how the Lord turns our sorrow to joy when he wrote, "You have turned for me my mourning into dancing; you have loosed my sackcloth and clothed me with gladness" (Psalm 30:11). So now, whenever I hear the Mourning Dove's sweet coo, I think of the joy that follows all who bring their sorrows to the Lord.

Birder's Journal

47. Like A Eagle

Morning Song: *"but those who hope in the Lord will renew their strength. They will soar on wings like eagles; they will run and not grow weary, they will walk and not be faint"*
(Isaiah 40:31)

Winging Through the Word
Read: Isaiah 40:10-31

Thoughts on the Fly
God is so vast, infinite, and beyond our level of comprehension that there are really no words adequate to describe him. But God wants to be known by us and to reveal himself to all who desire to know him. That's why he gave us his Word and that is why, in his Word, he gives us so many small glimpses of himself by comparing some of his attributes with various aspects of his creation. One of my favorites is the eagle. He told us, "I carried you on eagles' wings and brought you to myself" (Exodus 19:4). When I read those words my mind returns to the sight of a mother eagle soaring over her nest as she keeps a watchful eye on her young eaglets. Like an eagle, the Lord continually hovers over us with great power and wings of protection.

I visited the eagle's nest I had discovered several times over the summer months watching the young eagles grow, mature, and finally try to stretch their own wings. One morning when I got there, there were no eagles in the nest. But a few minutes later both of the young eagles landed on the edge of the nest. They had been out for a little test run. I didn't see the mother bird that morning but I am sure she spotted me. I know that the male and female eagle will both remain within about a mile from the nest for as long as their young ones are there. As I watched the young eagles now sitting contentedly back on their nest, I was reminded that we are created in our Father's imagine. As we grow in him, we will become more like him. We too, will be able to soar like young eagles.

Birder's Journal

48. The Hollywood Bird

Morning Song: "... everyone who is called
by my name, whom I created for
my glory, whom I formed and made"
(Isaiah 43:7)

Winging Through the Word
Read: Isaiah 43:1-15

Thoughts on the Fly
There's nothing quite as nice in the morning, especially for
someone who would rather sleep in, than waking up to the
melodious sound of finches outside our window. They flock
to our thistle feeder (literally) year-round but once spring
has arrived the windows get opened, and the finch boys go to
extra lengths to let the girls know they are available with their
beautiful and complex songs. There are three closely related
species of "red finches" that include the House Finch, Purple
Finch and Cassin's Finch. While the name "House Finch"
may sound a little boring, the story of how they got here is
anything but. The House Finch was native to Mexico but in
the early 1900s dealers started selling them in the US under
the much more glamorous name of "Hollywood Finches".
In the 1940's due to stricter laws in pet sales dealers released

most of their Hollywood Finches on Long Island. The colorful birds started breeding and soon spread across most of the eastern US. Today, they are common at most feeders. But to this musician's ear, their lovely song is anything but common.

While the pet store owners' motivations in renaming their birds were strictly monetary there is something to be said for having a name that gains attention and respect. We all know of individuals whose family name gives them prestige and importance simply by association. While most of us will never have that kind of name, we can all have something of infinitely greater worth. Each of us has been invited to become a member of God's family and to be named after our Creator and Savior. All who join their lives to his become bearers of "the name that is above every name" (Phil. 2:9). That is the name of Jesus.

Birder's Journal

Morning Song: *"Can a woman forget her nursing child . . . Even these may forget, yet I will not forget you"* (Isaiah 49:15)

Winging Through the Word
Read: Isaiah 49:1-16

Thoughts on the Fly

We watched in wonder as the mother robin sat on her four blue eggs. We felt like proud grandparents when we finally saw four little fuzz heads popping up over the edge of the nest. While Mom Robin's life might have been a little boring up to this point, it suddenly became a nearly 24-hour a day feeding frenzy that began from the moment the fuzz heads (who looked like about 80% mouth) arrived. She and the male robin took turns making worm runs to keep up with four insatiable appetites. But they both always remained within sight of the nest and if anything came within several yards of the nest they would go on the attack. One robin would fly away, loudly chattering to draw attention away from the nest. The other would sit on the ground nearby and start making a raucous warning sound. If the perceived threat (like someone with a camera) got too close, the aerial assaults and dive bombings would begin. The robins would allow nothing to come between them and their chicks even if it meant risking their own lives to do so.

It is obviously quite natural for a mother bird to defend her babies even to her own death. No wonder the Lord used that illustration to describe the way he cares for his beloved children. But his love goes far beyond that of a mother bird or a mother anything. We are told, "For one will scarcely die for a righteous person—though perhaps for a good person one would dare even to die—but God shows his love for us in that while we were still sinners, Christ died for us" (Rom. 5:7-8). His kind of love is not natural at all. You might say it is supernatural.

Birder's Journal

50. Winged Migration

Morning Song: *Who are these that fly along like clouds, like doves to their nests?*
(Isaiah 60:8)

Winging Through the Word
Read: Isaiah 60:1-22

Thoughts on the Fly

I love that sound. We hear their gentle quacking from our window throughout the spring, summer, and fall. But once the lake freezes over, the ambient quacking of the mallard ducks goes silent as our fair weather friends head south. It is actually only the females that quack. The males have a different one or two note call they only use during courtship. One could make comparisons to the human male/female conversational patterns . . . but I won't. Mallards will winter as far north as there is open water. They form pairs in the winter and then start their migration northward as early as midwinter heading for the female's place of origin. They arrive at nesting grounds in March or early April and build a nest in which to add their 8–10 eggs. The female will soon be left with the task of raising the chicks by herself. No wonder she quacks. She will lead the hatchlings to water as soon as their soft, downy feathers are dry. She can be seen with her ducklings in tow at their various stages of growth any time from May into July. In early fall, they will start for their wintering grounds, beginning the cycle all over again.

As I write, we are still awaiting the return of our mallard duck friends. We are also awaiting another migration. Isaiah was writing to a nation that was in shambles. Their city was completely destroyed and their people were carried into exile. He was reminding them (and us) of a coming day when the Lord would restore his people to their land. Such a day of joy it will be. But he was also speaking of a future time when each of us will make one more migration to the place where we will "possess the land forever".

Birder's Journal

51. Never Destroyed

Morning Song*: In those days no one will be hurt or destroyed on my holy mountain (Isaiah 65:25)*

Winging Through the Word
Read: Isaiah 65:17-25

Thoughts on the Fly

They say it might already be extinct. But they aren't sure. The Ivory-billed Woodpecker is one of the largest wood-peckers in the world, at 20 inches long with a wingspan of 30 inches. It has sometimes been confused with the Pileated Woodpecker but has slightly different markings. The species was thought to be extinct for most of the 20th century until it was possibly rediscovered in 2004. There was a reported sighting of a male Ivory-billed Woodpecker in Arkansas which was investigated and published in 2005 by the Cornell Lab of Ornithology. In 2006, a team of ornithologists from Auburn University reported sightings of Ivory-billed Wood-peckers in northwest Florida. There have been no sightings since then. In 2006 a $10,000 reward was offered for informa-tion leading to the discovery of an Ivory-billed Woodpecker nest or roost. In 2008 the Cornell Lab offered $50,000 to anyone who could lead them to a living Ivory-billed Wood-pecker. No one could. The American Birding Association currently lists the Ivory-billed Woodpecker as a Class 6 species: "definitely or probably extinct". Today, the Ivory-billed Woodpecker is often referred to as the "Holy Grail" of Ornithology.

It is very sad to think that such an amazing bird, or any bird or animal specials for that matter, is extinct. But that is unfortunately a reality of life on this planet. It is also a reminder of our responsibility to care for God's earth and his creatures as best we can. But the Bible also speaks of a day when nothing will ever be destroyed or go extinct again. When the Lord returns, there will be a new heaven and a new earth where peace (and Jesus) will reign, and life will be ever-lasting. One can't help but to wonder if we might even see the Ivory-billed Woodpecker.

Birder's Journal

52. The Swan Pond

Morning Song: *For as the new heavens and the new earth that I make shall remain before me, says the Lord, so shall your offspring and your name remain (Isaiah 66:22)*

Winging Through the Word
Read: Isaiah 66:10-23

Thoughts on the Fly

A small village not far from our home has a swan pond that is filled with ducks, fish and, of course, two beautiful white swans, Manny and Faye. It was the talk of the town (actually the talk of Central New York) when Faye laid her eggs on the nest that she and Manny had built there in the enclosed swan pond area. We were all anticipating the thought of swan babies (cygnets) and then the unthinkable occurred. Someone climbed over the fence, stole and then destroyed all seven of the swan eggs. Even though the person was caught and convicted we all remained devastated. All of us except Manny and Faye. The two swans created a new nest and Faye laid a second clutch of eggs only 10 days after the first ones were destroyed. And less than two months later, we all celebrated the arrival of four healthy cygnets, LaVerne, Holly,

Bella, and Dazzle. Thousands of visitors came to watch as they grew into healthy and beautiful white swans just like their presumably proud parents.

There was quite understandably a cry for justice against the person who so heartlessly destroyed the eggs of such lovely creatures. We wonder how people can do the evil things that they do, not just to animals but to each other as well. The Bible assures us that the Lord will repay the evil done to his creatures and to his children. There will be just punishment for the wicked and comfort for all of his people —for all who love him. But as Isaiah explains, he will also ultimately bring restoration to all of the earth. In his recreated new heaven and new earth we are told that peace like a river will reign and every living creature will worship him.

Birder's Journal

53. Appointed Seasons

Morning Song: *Even the stork in the sky knows her appointed seasons, and the dove, the swift and the thrush observe the time of their migration (Jeremiah 8:7 NIV)*

Winging Through the Word
Read: Ecclesiastes 3:1-14

Thoughts on the Fly

I was running late, but as I got out of my car I stopped abruptly and looked to the sky. The Canada Geese were flying overhead in their V-shaped formation honking as they went. I smiled. Even though snow was still on the ground, and the lake was frozen over, the return of the Canada Geese was a joyful reminder that the seasons were changing. The Canada Goose is a large wild goose with a black head and neck, white patches on the face and a brown body. For us northerners, it is also a clear sign of spring. They winter in the lower US and Mexico. In the spring they return to the northern US and Canada. The geese follow the same route each year, return to their same nesting signs, and even land at the same rest areas on way. In the fall, those who leave first tend to spend less time at their rest stops and get back home faster. The later ones usually spend more time at rest stops. Canada Geese migrate anywhere from 2000 to 3000 miles, travel anywhere from 40 to 70 mph, and can fly as many 1500 miles in 24 hours.

The Prophet Jeremiah makes reference to the instincts God gave his migratory creatures. He has given each of them a GPS system that is simply remarkable. Jeremiah was comparing the birds to God's people who seemed to have lost their way. They had forgotten the God who created them. In Ecclesiastes, we are reminded that there is a time and season for everything. The Canada Geese were designed to migrate each season. We were created to weep, to laugh, to mourn, to dance, and to follow the GPS he has put in every heart to guide us straight to him.

Birder's Journal

54. Outdoing Himself

Morning Song: *On the mountain height of Israel will I plant it, that it may bear branches and produce fruit and become a noble cedar. And under it will dwell every kind of bird; in the shade of its branches birds of every sort will nest (Ezekiel 17:23)*

Winging Through the Word
Read: Ezekiel 17:11-24

Thoughts on the Fly

He was one of the most extravagantly beautiful birds I had ever seen. The wood duck's colors and markings were so spectacular that he reminded me more of a work of art than a living creature. But then, he really is both. The wood duck is considered one of the most beautiful ducks in North America. He has a crested iridescent green and purple head with a white stripe leading from the eye to the crest, and another white stripe from the bill to the crest. The throat is white and the chest is burgundy with white flecks. The bill is brightly patterned black, white and red. The Creator really outdid himself on this bird. Wood ducks get their name because they build their nests in the cavities of trees.

They also have a rather unique habit called "dump nesting" where they will lay their eggs in another wood duck's nest. Female wood ducks observe other hens entering cavities to lay eggs and then do the same. Hens that dump eggs will often incubate their own eggs later in the nesting season. So, you might say they don't "put all their eggs in one basket" which makes it possible for more eggs to survive.

Ezekiel describes God's punishment of a bad and disobedient king. But God is not dependent on a human king to provide for his people. He will always have a plan—a remnant—of people who remain faithful so when one fails him (even if that one is a king), he has not put all his eggs in that basket. The Bible shows over and over again that God's people will survive even if they are temporarily dumped into a place they had not anticipated. But more than just survive. For them, he will outdo himself.

Birder's Journal

_____

_____

_____

_____

_____

_____

_____

_____

_____

_____

_____

_____

_____

_____

Morning Song: *The birds roost on its fallen trunk,
and the wild animals lie among its branches
(Ezekiel 31:13)*

Winging Through the Word
Read: Ezekiel 31:1-14

Thoughts on the Fly

I heard a woodpecker drumming on a tree outside our camp.
It was a performance that would have put Buddy Rich to
shame. I looked out the window and caught my breath. A
giant Pileated Woodpecker was drumming on a dead tree
right outside the window. The Pileated Woodpecker is one
of the largest woodpeckers in North America. It is a black,
crow-sized bird with a zebra-striped head and neck, and a
flaming red crest. It has a very distinctive "whinnying" call
that reminds me of the jungle. But the sound most often
associated with the Pileated Woodpecker is its incessant
drumming. They whack at dead trees and logs in search of
carpenter ants. They use their long, sticky tongues to poke
into the holes and drag out the ants. They also drum to get
the attention of potential mates (and judging from the

volume they can produce, I would guess this is quite effective for them).

As I watched from the window, a second Pileated Woodpecker landed on the same tree and joined the concert. I wondered if they had happened upon an ant fest or if the female bird was drumming up a little attention of her own. Couples are known to establish their own territory and then live there all year long often building nests in one of the holes they had hammered. I was excited about the prospects of new neighbors even if they were a little noisy. The Lord used the illustration of a dead tree like the one the woodpeckers had discovered to describe a nation that had become proud and did not acknowledge its strength had come from him. We can find hope in knowing that our God is more powerful than any enemy we face. That's definitely worth drumming about!

Birder's Journal

56. Extravagant Love

Morning Song: *Therefore, behold, I will allure her, and bring her into the wilderness, and speak tenderly to her (Hosea 2:14)*

Winging Through the Word
Read: Hosea 2:7-23

Thoughts on the Fly

He's an extravagant sight any time of year, but when a male Hooded Merganser is looking for women (mergansers, that is), he is a sight to behold. There are three different species of mergansers in North America that include the Common, the Red-breasted, and the Hooded Merganser. While the latter is the smallest of the three, I would have to say they are the most impressive little packages. They are small diving ducks with a thin bill and a fan-shaped, collapsible crest. The males are black above, with a white breast and chestnut flanks. The females are gray and brown. Hooded Mergansers are fairly common on small ponds and rivers, where they can be seen diving for fish and seizing it in their thin, serrated bills. The males are best identified by the large white patch on their crest that varies in size when the crest is raised or lowered.

They court the females by expanding their white, sail-like crests and by making very low, gravelly, groaning calls.

While the male merganser attempts to dazzle its mate with its impressive white crest and seductive calls, the Bible uses similar imagery to describe how the Lord seeks to draw each of us to himself. He compares himself to a lover seeking to draw his beloved back to himself even though she has been unfaithful to him. And indeed he is the ultimate lover. We are told that "God is love" and that he desires to draw all people to himself. Not with a white crest, but definitely with songs of love. He told us that "…he will rejoice over you with gladness; he will quiet you by his love; he will exult over you with loud singing" (Zeph. 3:17). One would have to call that kind of love extravagant.

Birder's Journal

_____

_____

_____

_____

_____

_____

_____

_____

_____

_____

_____

_____

_____

_____

_____

_____

_____

57. The Bluebird of Happiness

Morning Song: *"But for you who fear my name, the sun of righteousness shall rise with healing in its wings" (Malachi 4:2)*

Winging Through the Word
Read: Malachi 4

Thoughts on the Fly

I'm a little embarrassed to admit this but the first time I saw one, I initially thought it was a miniature robin (there is no such thing, by the way). I didn't know that a bluebird has an orange breast. I've since learned that, like the American Robin, the Eastern Bluebird is a member of the Thrush family. When I finally realized I was looking at my very first bluebird, I was very happy. Which made me think about the expression, "The Bluebird of Happiness". Which made me wonder where that expression came from. I'm not sure I conclusively found the answer, but I did learn that there was a Nobel winning play by Maurice Maeterlinck in the early 1900s based on a fairytale about a bluebird. And Judy Garland sang about a bluebird in 1939 in "Somewhere Over the Rainbow". But the most interesting story I found came from Native American Folklore. According to the Cochiti tribe, the firstborn son of the Sun was named Bluebird. The Navajos sing the Bluebird Song to remind tribe members to wake at dawn and rise to greet the sun.

Interestingly, the Old Testament ends on a note of promise and hope. You might even call it a sunrise. Malachi's mention of the sun of righteous was none other than the promised Messiah—the Light of the World of whom Isaiah wrote, "The people who walked in darkness have seen a great light; those who dwelt in a land of deep darkness, on them has light shone . . . you have increased its joy; they rejoice before you as with joy at the harvest" (Isaiah 9:2,3). I'm still not sure what the origins are of the bluebird of happiness but I do know that the firstborn Son is the source of everlasting joy.

Birder's Journal

58. Not to Worry

Morning Song: *Look at the birds. They don't plant or harvest or store food in barns, for your heavenly Father feeds them. And aren't you far more valuable to him than they are? (Matthew 6:26)*

Winging Through the Word
Read: Matt 6:19-34

Thoughts on the Fly

I recently read an article that has inspired me to do a little family planning this year. It is almost nesting season and I read that one way to attract birds to nest in the area is to help them out a little bit with some free housing supplies. After pushing aside any unfounded concerns I may have had about creating a welfare state, I learned that one can make a little birdie care package of nesting materials, put them in a suet cage and hang them from a tree out in the yard. It would make sense that if birds found an easy and affordable place to purchase their building materials they would pick a location for the nest that would make the commute as short as possible. Materials could include bits of yarn, string or twine, pine needles, grass clippings, pet or human hair, or cotton batting. One should be careful to avoid anything treated with chemicals, and lint from the dryer was also discouraged. Finally, be sure that the supplies are in small enough pieces to be easily pulled from the suet cage and carried in their beaks.

It is fun to think that we humans can make life a little easier for our feathered friends and even have some say in where they decide to take up residence. I can't help thinking that God smiles when he sees us taking on the role of benevolent provider. After all, he has not only been providing for the birds since the beginning of creation, but has also been providing for us. In fact, Jesus used the illustration of how he feeds the birds so faithfully to assure us that he will, all the more, care for each of the needs we bring to our loving heavenly Father.

Birder's Journal

Morning Song: *Thus you will recognize them by their fruits (Matthew 7:20)*

Winging Through the Word
Read: Matthew 7: 7-25

Thoughts on the Fly

When a finch showed up at our new birdhouse I grabbed our bird identification book and quickly identified it as a purple finch. Even though it was red, not purple (who gets to name birds, anyway?). I told a friend that we had seen a purple finch and she asked if I was sure. She explained that there are actually three kinds of red-colored finches and while they look quite similar, the house finch is much more common than the purple finch in our area. The differences in appearance are very subtle so distinguishing between house finches and purple finches can be a challenge even for experienced birders. Even knowing what those slight differences were, I was still not sure which of the two finches we had at our feeder. Then one day up at our camp, I saw a purple finch. And, yes, I would have to say he even looked a little bit purple. I then realized the finches at home had to be house finches. Mystery solved.

While telling finches apart can difficult, the Bible speaks of a similar challenge in telling true followers of God from false teachers. The two groups often look quite a bit alike. The differences, at least outwardly, can be subtle. Jesus told his followers to not judge someone by outward appearance but to look at the kind of fruit being produced by their lives. The best way to identify an imposter is to know the real thing. As soon as I saw a purple finch I knew how to recognize the house finch. When we know someone who really loves the Lord it is much easier to recognize someone who is faking it. It really is all about the fruit of love (I wonder if it comes in purple).

Birder's Journal

60. Priceless

Morning Song: *Are not two sparrows sold for a penny? Yet not one of them will fall to the ground outside your Father's care (Matt. 10:29)*

Winging Through the Word
Read: Matthew 10:16-30

Thoughts on the Fly

Most of us think of sparrows as being the most common-place and uninteresting little birds at our feeders. In reality, the sparrow family comprises over 140 different species world-wide and comes in a wide variety of different colors, shades and markings. In general, sparrows are small, chubby brown-gray birds with short tails and short beaks. In the United States, some of the most common sparrows are the Chipping Sparrows (known for the "chipping" sound that they make), the Song Sparrows (who live up to their name with their lovely songs), White-Throated Sparrows, Fox Sparrows, Field Sparrows and House Sparrows. The House Sparrow is one of the newer species on the scene having been brought from Europe and introduced into New York City's Central Park in 1850. Today they can be found all over North

119

America. They are not picky eaters and are known to eat over 830 different foods. Though they are not water birds, House Sparrows have been observed swimming underwater to escape from a trap. Since they aren't normally water birds, they prefer to bathe themselves in dust throwing soil and dust over themselves as though they were taking a bath in water.

Despite all those abilities and interesting habits, for the most part sparrows are still considered to be rather unimportant and of little worth to most people. Apparently things weren't much different about 2000 years ago. Jesus used the illustration of the common sparrow, not to show of how little value they are, but to show of how great value we are to him. The God who created and cares for even the most insignificant little bird cares infinitely more for each of us. In fact, he cared enough to give his very life for us. In his eyes that makes us priceless.

Birder's Journal

61. The Ultimate Protection

Morning Song: *. . . how often I have longed to gather your children together, as a hen gathers her chicks under her wings, and you were not willing (Matthew 23:37)*

Winging Through the Word
Read: Matthew 23:25-39

Thoughts on the Fly

When he was a little boy my husband had a pet chicken named Icky. He raised Icky from birth after hatching him from an egg in his homemade cigar box incubator. Needless to say, he loved his little pet. But sadly Icky became the original KFC one day when their henhouse burned down. Hearing about Icky's fate reminded me of another chicken story I once heard. It was a parable written to illustrate God's love and protection for all of his children. As the story goes, a forest ranger was walking through the fields after a forest fire had devastated the area. He found the petrified remains of a bird. When he attempted to move the bird's body with a stick, three chicks scurried out from under the mother bird's charred wings. She had gathered them underneath herself so that even though she died in the fire, all of her chicks survived. This modern day parable was used to illustrate the love of Christ who sacrificed his life on the cross to save the lives of all who find cover in him.

Jesus also used the illustration of a mother hen in describing the love he has for his people. As he looked over the city of Jerusalem just days prior to his death he knew that they, too, were facing imminent destruction. The sorrow he felt for them, and for all of humankind, was what motivated him to continue on his journey into the city knowing he would soon be nailed to a cross. But he also went there with the joy of knowing his death would not be in vain. Instead, he was about to spread his wings over everyone who comes to him by faith knowing that in him, they will find protection and eternal life.

Birder's Journal

62. Tree of Life

Morning Song: *Yet when planted, it grows and becomes the largest of all garden plants, with such big branches that the birds can perch in its shade (Mark 4:32)*

Winging Through the Word
Read: Mark 4:10-34

Thoughts on the Fly

We have a beautiful cedar tree in our backyard. What is most amazing is that I had purchased our lovely *Thuja Plicata* by mail about 10 years ago. It arrived as not much more than a stick with a few branches on it. Today, it is the tallest tree in the area and its branches are almost constantly filled with birds. It is no doubt because of the cedar tree that we have so many birds at our feeders as they go to and from the tree finding safety in its branches. The *Thuja Plicata* is also known as the *Giant Arborvitae.* Arborvitae is Latin for "tree of life". It was named by the French explorer Jacques Cartier in 1536 while sailing up the St. Lawrence River with a crew suffering from scurvy. The Native Americans gave them a cure that was made from the branches of the tree. The crew rapidly went from near death to being completely healed. Hence, Cartier named it the Tree of Life.

Jesus compared the Kingdom of God to a tiny mustard seed that grew into a giant tree the birds could perch on. What started as a handful of disciples would one day be a countless sea of believers worshiping at the throne of God in Heaven. And in the glimpse of that wondrous place we have been given, we discover the very Tree that Jacques Cartier was referring to. We are told about "the tree of life with its twelve kinds of fruit, yielding its fruit each month. The leaves of the tree were for the healing of the nations" (Rev. 22:3). Our cedar tree is a constant reminder of the day when we will be free from all illness and suffering—free to join the crowd and worship Jesus.

Birder's Journal

63. Fast Food

Photo courtesy John Benson

Morning Song: *But he answered them,
"You give them something to eat" (Mark 6:37)*

Winging Through the Word
Read: Mark 6:30-44

Thoughts on the Fly
The small bay behind our camp is a marvelous place to look
for wildlife. The still shallow waters are the perfect place for
birds of all kinds to come and dine. One of our neighbors
took that advantage even further by building a small bird
house and placing it on a pole right in the middle of the bay.
So, once or twice a year we get to watch a tree swallow family
raise their young. Tree Swallows are about five inches long.
The adult has iridescent blue-green upperparts, white under
parts, and a very slightly forked tail. Swallows spend most of
their time in flight even scooping water to drink while flying.
They live on flying insects and are one of the few birds that
catch and eat their prey in flight (which gives new meaning
to "fast food"). Swallow parents teach their young to hunt
on their own by transferring an insect to the young swallow from beak to beak while in flight. Then the parent drops

insects for the young bird to catch. Soon, the young swallows are able to catch their own insects.

It is fascinating to watch how the swallows first care for their young then creatively teach them to become independent and provide for themselves. When a hungry crowd of over 5000 people needed to be fed, Jesus used it as an opportunity to teach his disciples a valuable lesson. He told them to feed the crowds using the meager supplies they had, combined with the power of the God they served. They learned the lesson well. This same group of disciples would one day go forth in the power of his Spirit and provide the entire world with the message of hope and salvation that can only be found in him.

Birder's Journal

_____

_____

_____

_____

_____

_____

_____

_____

_____

_____

_____

_____

_____

_____

_____

_____

_____

_____

64. Birds of the Ground

Morning Song: *But she answered him, "Yes, Lord; yet even the dogs under the table eat the children's crumbs" (Mark 7:28)*

Winging Through the Word
Read: Mark 7:24-30

Thoughts on the Fly
When I first saw one, I thought it looked like a little black bird that had jumped in a bowl of bleach. Juncos are now year-round guests at our feeders. Though, that's not quite correct. They are year-round guests *below* our feeders. They prefer eating the seeds that have spilled from the feeders rather than eating out of the feeders. Dark-eyed Juncos are members of the sparrow family. They are easy to recognize by their white bellies that end sharply below the neck of an otherwise black body. In addition, they have white tail feathers that flash in flight. Juncos are also known for eating off of the ground, from forest floors or, like ours, on lawns under birdfeeders. One description I read referred to them as "birds of the ground." One could laugh at the thought that just a

few feet over their heads they could be eating their fill at the feeders but that they actually prefer the "leftovers".

Our Juncos remind me of the story of a woman who came to Jesus because her daughter was being tormented by a demon. At that point in his ministry, Jesus had not yet gone to the Non-Jewish people. But that was not going to deter this desperate mother. When Jesus playfully told her that it was not right to take away the children's bread and give it to the dogs, she immediately replied that even the dogs are allowed to eat the crumbs that have fallen on the ground. The woman had such great faith that she knew even the tiniest morsel given to her from God would be enough to heal her daughter. She was right. Jesus told her, "For this statement . . . the demon has left your daughter." Maybe the Juncos are on to something!

Birder's Journal

65. Do Unto Others

Morning Song: *"give, and it will be given to you. Good measure, pressed down, shaken together, running over, will be put into your lap. For with the measure you use it will be measured back to you"*
(Luke 6:38)

Winging Through the Word
Read: Luke 6:20-37

Thoughts on the Fly
We started with a very simple hummingbird feeder. But it wasn't long before we upgraded to a more elaborate feeder with six feeding stations so that we could accommodate several guests at a time. It seemed like a great idea, but there was one problem we had not anticipated. Our first guest was a beautiful male ruby-throated hummingbird with a brilliant green iridescent body and fiery red neck. He gave each of the petals a try and even landed on one for a good long drink. Then he flew to a nearby branch for a little break. Suddenly, two more hummers appeared on the scene—a female and another male. They had hardly arrived before I heard a loud twittering sound and Ruby-the-First swooped down on them in what appeared to be a bit of a tantrum driving both of the new arrivals away.

Then he twittered his way back to his branch where one could only assume he was gloating over his easy victory. Despite being the smallest birds in the world, hummingbirds are known to be extremely territorial and aggressive. And from what I saw, they are very good at it.

While aggressive and territorial behavior is perfectly acceptable for hummingbirds (unless you are the other hummingbird), it just doesn't work that way for us humans. For us, it is the exact opposite response that brings us the biggest blessings. We are told to do to others as we would want them to do to us. We are also told that the more we give away, the more we will receive. That doesn't necessarily mean we'll always get the best spot at the hummingbird feeder but it does mean we will be blessed in this life and the next, with all of the things that matter most.

Birder's Journal

66. His Eye on the Sparrow

Photo courtesy ForestWanderer.com

Morning Song: *Are not five sparrows sold for two pennies? And not one of them is forgotten before God (Luke 12:6)*

Winging Through the Word
Read: Luke 12:1-12

Thoughts on the Fly

It is interesting that one of the most common, least appreciated little birds is the one that Jesus made into a superstar in the New Testament. Despite their lack of popularity, sparrows prefer to live near humans. I wonder if God made them that way, in part, so he could use them as an illustration of his love for us. Jesus repeatedly pointed to the sparrow and described how valuable even the most overlooked and insignificant of his creatures are, and how much more valuable each of us are to him, no matter how overlooked and insignificant we feel. His words were also the source of inspiration behind the lovely old hymn, "His Eye is on the Sparrow". In 1905, Civilla Martin wrote the lyrics to this hymn that have encouraged countless others ever since: "Why should I feel discouraged, why should the shadows come, Why should my heart be lonely, and long for heaven and home, When Jesus is my portion? My constant friend is He: His eye is on the sparrow, and I know He watches me".

She described the story behind the song: "Early in the spring of 1905, my husband and I were sojourning in Elmira, New York. We contracted a deep friendship for a couple by the name of Mr. and Mrs. Doolittle, true saints of God. Mrs. Doolittle had been bedridden for nigh twenty years. Her husband was an incurable cripple… in a wheel chair. Despite their afflictions, they lived happy Christian lives, bringing inspiration and comfort to all who knew them. One day while we were visiting with the Doolittles, my husband commented on their bright hopefulness and asked them for the secret of it. Mrs. Doolittle's reply was simple: 'His eye is on the sparrow, and I know He watches me'."

Birder's Journal

67. Small Packages

Morning Song: *And he was seeking to see who Jesus was, but on account of the crowd he could not, because he was small in stature (Luke 19:3)*

Winging Through the Word
Read: Luke 19:1-10

Thoughts on the Fly

They were so tiny that when I first spotted them bobbing on the water I wasn't sure exactly what they were. Then, as I watched, they all disappeared below the surface only to collectively reappear a few moments later. I grabbed my binoculars hoping for a closer look to identify the cute little birds. Once I had them in focus it was obvious that a flock of buffleheads had made a stopover on our small lake, on their way north for the summer. Buffleheads are small, chubby diving ducks. They are also known as butterballs. Males appear to be black-and white from a distance. They have a large dark glossy green and purple head with a striking white patch. Females are gray-brown with a smaller white patch on the cheek. Buffleheads are the smallest diving ducks in North America. But what they lack in size, they make up for in energy. Buffleheads are almost continually in motion either swimming along the water's surface or abruptly diving and resurfacing as they eat. They give meaning to the expression, "good things come in small packages".

The cute and energetic little buffleheads remind me of another small package found in a man who Jesus encountered one day. Zacchaeus didn't by any means start out as a good man (he was actually a tax collector). However, after this vertically challenged individual had an encounter with Jesus, he went from being a "wee little man" (as the old children's song goes), to becoming a kind and generous man filled with the love of God. His newfound faith didn't do anything for his physical stature, but it did take him to all new heights. Zacchaeus went from being a tiny tax collector to becoming a saved sinner and a very good man in a small package.

Birder's Journal

68. Known By Its Voice

Morning Song: *When he has brought out all his own, he goes before them, and the sheep follow him, for they know his voice (John 10:4)*

Winging Through the Word
Read: John 10:1-18

Thoughts on the Fly

We heard the first yodel from inside our camp. As we stepped out onto the porch, we heard it answered from across the river. The two loons were apparently having an intense conversation. The yodel is the most complex call of the Common Loon's repertoire. It is a loud call that is only used by males to defend their territory. We were obviously observing some kind of territorial dispute as the two loons answered back and forth over the dark waters. The yodel starts with three notes, much like the wail, and then ends with several repeated swinging phrases. What is most fascinating is that each individual loon has its own unique vocal signature encoded into its yodel. So, a male loon can be identified by its yodel. Since the purpose of the yodel is to defend a specific territory, if a male moves to a different territory, he will change his yodel.

The loon's yodel is not only a highly complex method of communication but also shows the unique identity of each of these delightful creatures.

God chose to build personal identification into much of his creation, and especially in us humans. We can be identified by our DNA, our fingerprints and, yes, even by our vocal imprint. He has made each of us as unique individuals who are personally known (and loved) by him. The Lord has told us that he, too, can be known by his voice. He calls to each of us—not in protection of his territory but to invite us to enter in. Once we have chosen to follow his voice he will passionately defend us as our protective Father and, as he has promised, "no one will snatch them out of my hand" (Jn 10:28). That's definitely something to yodel about.

Birder's Journal

69. No Place like Home

Morning Song: *And if I go and prepare a place for you, I will come again and will take you to myself, that where I am you may be also (John 14:3)*

Winging Through the Word
Read: John 14:1-21

Thoughts on the Fly

We have a competition going on with the neighbors up at our camp. To be honest, I'm not even sure our neighbors are aware of that fact. But for the past several years I have been determined to make sure that the wrens build their nest in our birdhouse (as opposed to any other birdhouses in the immediate vicinity). We have a lovely lighthouse-shaped birdhouse in our yard. Our neighbors have one shaped like a chili pepper. The choice should be obvious. The House Wren is named, in part, because of its preference for human-made birdhouses. Though, wrens are known for all kinds of eccentric choices of nesting sites including cow skulls, flower pots, tin cans, boots, scarecrows, and the pockets of hanging laundry. Wrens are small brown birds with a long pointed bill. They are perhaps best recognized for their beautiful and melodious song of multiple loud notes rapidly ascending then descending in pitch. The male builds the nest and actually makes several nests in the area to attract the female and to give her the option to choose between them all. When the female arrives she inspects all of the nests and then chooses the one she likes best.

The male wren will do whatever it takes to attract the female to choose his nest (hopefully in my birdhouse). Much like Mr. Wren, Jesus has built a place in his kingdom for each of us. Before he left to join his father in heaven after his death and resurrection he told his disciples, "In my Father's house are many mansions: if it were not so, I would have told you. I go to prepare a place for you" (John 14:2 KJV). And I can assure you, the place he is preparing will beat all of the competition.

Birder's Journal

70. Many Languages

Morning Song: *And at this sound the multitude came together, and they were bewildered, because each one was hearing them speak in his own language (Acts 2:6)*

Winging Through the Word
Read: Acts 2:1-21

Thoughts on the Fly

I paused to listen to the robin . . . or . . . was it a finch? No, it was a sparrow . . . or was it a red-winged black bird? Suddenly, I realized I was listening to the varied songs of a mockingbird. The scientific name for the mockingbird is Mimus Polyglottos meaning "many-tongued mimic." Mockingbirds have been known to produce the songs of up to 39 different bird species in addition to other sounds such as dog barks and even some man-made devices such as musical instruments. Talk about being multi-lingual. As I listened, this little many-tongued mimic brought to mind a scene described in the Bible. The Lord had told his disciples to wait for him to send his Holy Spirit to them. As they gathered together to celebrate Pentecost, the Holy Spirit came as promised. Tongues of fire appeared on each disciple and they all began to speak in other languages as the Spirit enabled them. People who were visiting from all over the world were suddenly hearing their own language being spoken by these native Galileans. And what were they hearing? They exclaimed, ". . . we hear them telling in our own tongues the mighty works of God" (Acts 2:11).

I was amazed by the mockingbird's ability to so perfectly mimic other birds and creatures. Like the faithful believers at Pentecost, he was doing exactly what his Creator designed him to do. And in so doing, the mockingbird was declaring the wonders of God in his own unique way. Now, if God could use a wild bird to so gloriously testify of the wonders of his Creator, just think what he can do with each of us. When we speak, filled with his Holy Spirit and prompted by his love within us, others will be able to hear us declaring the wonders of God, and believe.

Birder's Journal

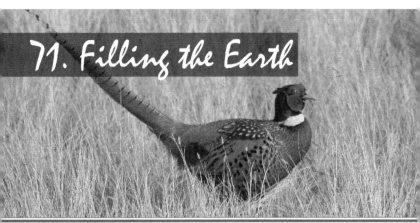

71. Filling the Earth

Photo courtesy Randy Lakes/USFWS

Morning Song: *But many of those who had heard the message believed; and the number of the men came to be about five thousand (Acts 4:4)*

Winging Through the Word
Read: Acts 4:1-21

Thoughts on the Fly

We saw a flash of motion at the side of the road and looked over just in time to see a magnificent ring-necked pheasant disappear into the brush. "What a beautiful bird!" I commended to my husband. Pheasants are both beautiful and plentiful throughout North America but like most of us, they are not native to the US. They are immigrants from China who somewhere along the way achieved the status of permanent resident. The ring-necked pheasant is a member of the same family as quails, partridges and chickens. The males are richly colored with blue-green heads, red face wattles, and white neck rings. Both sexes have long, pointed tails. They measure two to three feet long including their 20-inch tail. The first successful introduction of ring-necked pheasants to the US was in 1881 when Judge O.N. Denny (US consul to China) shipped several dozen Chinese ring-necks to his home in Oregon. Nine years later he released some into the wild. Today, despite many predators and hunters, pheasants can be found throughout North America in abundance. No game birds introduced to the US have been as successful as the ring-necked pheasant.

The abundant US pheasant population started with just a few birds. They are much like the early Church. After Christ's resurrection, he gave the responsibility of spreading the message of hope and life to a handful of disciples. And in the power of the Holy Spirit these bold men and women went forth, despite severe persecution, and filled the earth with Christ-followers. Upon the faith of a few, Jesus said he would build his church "and the gates of hell shall not prevail against it" (Matt. 16:18). In fact, the more opposition they face, the more his Church continues to grow even today just as Jesus promised.

Birder's Journal

72. MR Ducks

Morning Song: *Now when they saw the boldness of Peter and John, and perceived that they were uneducated, common men, they were astonished. And they recognized that they had been with Jesus (Acts 4:13)*

Winging Through the Word
Read: 1 Corinthians 1:18-30

Thoughts on the Fly

I have no idea where it originated, but once I heard the riddle, I never forgot it. In fact, every time I spot a duck, it goes through my mind. See if you can figure it out: "MR ducks! MR not ducks! OSAR! CDEDBD wings? MR ducks! YIB, MR ducks." When one thinks of ducks, one most commonly thinks of mallards. They are the most abundant duck in the world with nearly 10 million in North America alone. Mallards are called "dabblers" meaning that, unlike diving ducks, they have smaller feet (that's a hint for the riddle by the way) and their legs are situated farther forward. Dabblers skim food from the surface or in shallow water by tipping forward to submerge their heads and necks. They are very attractive and colorful birds. The male in particular is easily identified by its lavishly iridescent green head, white collar, greenish yellow bill and orange legs and feet. They are also sociable birds by nature easily adapting to humans. They are ancestors of the common white duck which explains, in part, why they are so domestic in nature. Mallards eat invertebrate and plants and are valuable in the wild for destroying mosquito larvae.

So, though mallards are considered common, they are anything but common in appearance, in benefit to the environment and in their friendly relationship with humans. In God's eyes, no human is considered common. He extends his offer of grace to even those who society writes off as insignificant and makes us into "a chosen race, a royal priesthood, a holy nation, a people for his own possession" (1 Peter 2:9). And once we have been filled with his Spirit we are of great value to our world and to our Savior. As for the mallards, 'Em are ducks!

Birder's Journal

73. Upside Down

Morning Song: *"…These men who have turned the world upside down have come here also"*
(Acts 17:6)

Winging Through the Word
Read: Acts 17:1-16

Thoughts on the Fly
Its nickname is "The Upside Down Bird". One would only need to watch the White-breasted Nuthatch for a matter of minutes to understand how it got the name. The feature that most distinguishes this animated little bird is its habit of creeping head first up and down trees. Because of its entertaining acrobatics, the nuthatch is a favorite at many birdfeeders. Our nuthatches enjoy suet in the winter, and sunflower or safflower seeds in the summer. When they eat from either feeder they seem entirely obvious as to whether they are facing up or hanging completely upside down. They seem to hop along tree branches just as easily in either direction using their long rear claws. The nuthatch earned its name because of its habit of wedging a large seed or insect in a crack and hacking at it with its strong bill. Like the chickadee, the nuthatch will usually grab a seed from the feeder and

hop to another location to "hatch" and eat it making a little beeping sound as it goes.

Being upside down is completely natural for the nut-hatch. One would be tempted to think that they are defying gravity as they walk along the bottom of branches. In the earliest days of the Church in the time shortly after Jesus returned to Heaven, the young believers were doing some acrobatics of their own. Even their enemies accused them of turning the world upside down. If you think about it, they started with a handful of disciples. Many were persecuted and even killed for their faith. The world tried to snuff the whole movement out but in the power of the Holy Spirit they, too, defied gravity and as they spread the Good News all over the world they truly did turn it upside down.

Birder's Journal

74. Responding Appropriately

Morning Song: *So he reasoned in the synagogue with the Jews and the devout persons, and in the market-place every day with those who happened to be there (Acts 17:17)*

Winging Through the Word
Read: Acts 17:16-31

Thoughts on the Fly

A small cluster of chickadees landed on the new suet just moments after I refilled the basket. That is, a small cluster of chickadees and one nuthatch with an orange-red breast. The Red-breasted Nuthatch is a tiny energetic bird that is known for its habit of coexisting with chickadees. Like other nut-hatches, it hops with ease up and down and underneath tree branches. It is a very vocal bird with a cute little "beep beep" call has been compared to tiny tin horns or a child's noise-maker, though it actually has a wide assortment of whistles, trills and calls. Apparently the bird is also a bit of a linguist since the Red-breasted Nuthatch is known for its unique ability to understand the calls of the chickadees it associates with. The chickadee has a number of complex calls that com-municate information about the size and risk of potential predators. While other species can recognize the simple alarm calls, only the Red-breasted Nuthatch can actually interpret the chickadees' various calls and respond accordingly. I guess that makes them bilingual.

It is fascinating that nuthatches have the ability to understand what their neighbors, the chickadees, are talking about. It is even more interesting to think that they can respond to what is communicated. When the Apostle Paul traveled to Athens, he went to the common marketplace and reasoned with the people there. He took the time to study their culture and understand their beliefs and then he responded appropriately. He took what they were familiar with, including one of their own pagan gods, and used it to point them to the "Lord of heaven and earth". And we are told that some of the listeners there in the marketplace joined him and believed. Now that is what I call an appropriate response.

Birder's Journal

75. True Colors

Morning Song: *Do not be conformed to this world, but be transformed by the renewal of your mind, that by testing you may discern what is the will of God, what is good and acceptable and perfect (Romans 12:2)*

Winging Through the Word
Read: Romans 12:1-21

Thoughts on the Fly
Our neighbor had a finch feeder outside her kitchen window. It was winter and I asked her if she was seeing any finches at this time of year. She commented that it was the strangest thing. All summer long the feeder was constantly filled with brilliant yellow goldfinches. But as soon as the weather started turning colder, the goldfinches disappeared and all she ever saw were some rather plain brown birds. I did my best to not burst out laughing. Apparently no one ever told her that those beautiful male goldfinches lose their color in the winter. The drab colored birds who took over her feeder were probably the same yellow birds who delighted her over the summer months. Those glorious colors come in very handy for the male goldfinches during the mating season

149

but there are some practical advantages to dressing down for winter. For one thing, they are less flashy and obvious to predators after they are done being flashy and obvious to the girls in spring. The females are less colorful all year round which helps to keep them less visible while sitting on their nests.

While there are good reasons for goldfinches to lose their color and blend in to their surroundings, those who love the Lord are discouraged from blending in with the rest of the world. Not that he wants us to wear flashy colors, but he does want us to stand out in how we live. We are told to be transformed from being like the world to being like him. We are to live and love like he does, to forgive as he has forgiven us, to remain thankful in our trials, and to overcome evil with good. That, according to our heavenly father, is how we show our true colors.

Birder's Journal

_____

_____

_____

_____

_____

_____

_____

_____

_____

_____

_____

_____

_____

_____

_____

76. Working Together

Morning Song: *So then neither he who plants is anything, nor he who waters, but God who gives the increase (1 Corinthians 3:7)*

Winging Through the Word
Read: 1 Corinthians 3:4-23

Thoughts on the Fly

I was out in my kayak stalking loons. I spotted one in the distance and began my careful stealth tactics only to discover, to my disappointment, it was only a cormorant. But when he took off, leaving a wake of splashes behind him, I had to admit he was a magnificent creature despite his bad reputation. The word "cormorant" is derived from the Latin term "corvus marinus" which means "sea crow". If you ask most fishermen they would agree that the cormorant is about as popular to them as the crow is to farmers. It is a large black bird with a long neck, long hooked bill and webbed feet set back on their bodies giving them the ability to do a strong forward thrust under water. That ability makes them expert divers, which also makes them expert fish catchers. And therein lies the problem. Fishermen not only see them as competition but also as a threat to the game fish population. No amount of good looks can compensate for that to a fisherman.

It is interesting that in China the fishermen have an entirely different take on cormorants. They train cormorants to catch fish for them wearing a neck ring to prevent them from swallowing what they catch. Well trained birds can even be sent out without the ring. Rather than working in competition, they work together. We can all learn a lesson from the Chinese fishermen. God wants his people to work together, too. Even though we all have different abilities and skills, he never meant for us to work in competition or, even worse, against each other. We are a team – his team – and when we pool our talents and our hearts, we will not only make great fishers (of men), but will change the world.

Birder's Journal

77. Being Attractive

Morning Song: *To the weak I became weak, to win the weak. I have become all things to all people so that by all possible means I might save some (1 Corinthians 9:22)*

Winging Through the Word
Read: 1 Corinthians 9:1-23

Thoughts on the Fly

Now that we are up to seven or eight feeders at home and another five or six at camp, we have learned that if you want to attract a specific kind of bird, you have to offer menu items that will appeal to that particular species. So, when we wanted to attract goldfinches, we put out a feeder with black thistle (Nyjer seed). To attract woodpeckers, we hung a suet container (and in the process we attracted nuthatches). For our hummingbirds, we hung up a hummingbird feeder with sugar water. We discovered that bluebirds love mealworms so we put out a feeder exclusively for them but ended up attracting wrens, too. When we started to get some birds (and squirrels) that we didn't want to attract, we replaced the "cheap" seeds with safflower seeds and suddenly found that feeder filled with cardinals, titmice, and house finches. We hung an entire sunflower out on top of one of the feeders and quickly made friends with a blue jay. Of course the seed that attracts the most variety is sunflower seed. So we always have plenty of that.

While our yard looks almost like a bird feeder garage sale, we love the variety of birds we get to enjoy all year long. You have to use the right kind of seeds if you want to attract birds to your feeders. The Apostle Paul worked under a very similar principle in helping the people he met to understand how much God loves them and to attract them to that Love. He always tried to avoid offense. He related to the poor in one way, and to the rich in other, to the "religious" in one way and the nonreligious in another. He did whatever he could to attract people to Jesus.

Birder's Journal

78. Grace and Skill

Morning Song: *On the contrary, the parts of the body that seem to be weaker are indispensable (1 Corinthians 12:22)*

Winging Through the Word
Read: 1 Corinthians 12:14-31

Thoughts on the Fly

Loons are magnificently beautiful water fowl that grow up to three feet in length. They feed mainly on fish and are extremely well equipped to do so. The loon swims gracefully on the surface and dives as well as any other bird. Their legs are built far back on their bodies enabling them to dive to depths of up to 200 feet. They can also fly at up to 75 mph. But there are a couple of things they can't do well. Because of the placement of their feet, they are clumsy and can't walk well on land. They also can't take off from the water without a fairly long "runway". They need anywhere from 30 yards up to quarter mile to be able to gain enough speed, while running across the top of the water, to take off. We have heard stories where loons had landed on small ponds and were stuck there, helpless to lift off without the aid of a human rescue team.

While they will not be winning any foot races God perfectly designed loons to dive as well as, if not better than, any other bird. On dry ground they would die but when they are in their element—on water—they swim and dive with unsurpassed grace and skill. God perfectly designed each of us with specific skills, abilities, talents and gifts. Like the loon that is clumsy and inept on dry land there are talents each of us simply don't have. Not everyone is a preacher or a worship leader for example. But everyone has been given a unique gift and a calling only they can fulfill. When we are in our element, using the gifts he has given us, whatever we do will be marked by unsurpassed grace and skill.

Birder's Journal

Morning Song: *The weapons we fight with are not the weapons of the world. On the contrary, they have divine power to demolish strongholds (2 Corinthians 10:4)*

Winging Through the Word
Read: 2 Corinthians 10:1-18

Thoughts on the Fly
The only Toucans I ever saw were at the zoo, on TV, or on a box of cereal (remember Toucan Sam?). Though they are native exclusively to the jungles of South and Central America, these two-foot tall birds with eight-inch colorful bills are recognized by almost everyone. They are brightly colored but in their tropical environment this actually serves as a good camouflage for them. Not that they seem concerned about secrecy. Toucans normally keep up a racket of calls and vocalizations, which would suggest that they aren't trying very hard to remain hidden. When they do decide to hide they can roll up into balls to make themselves smaller. But the feature they are best known for is their oversized beaks. They use them to reach fruit on branches that are too small to support their weight, and to skin their pickings. They also

use them to pitch food to one another during a mating ritual fruit toss. What they can't really use them for is as a weapon. It is a honeycomb of bone that is mostly made up of air. While its size may deter predators, it is of little use in combating them. So, it's all just for show.

Thankfully, the weapons the Lord gives to us are not just for show. We all know that this world can be a tough place to survive in, and we have some very real enemies working against us (Satan being the chief). The weapon we have been given is nothing less than the Holy Spirit himself. He lives in each of our hearts giving us the wisdom, guidance, and words we need. He also works all of our circumstances together to bring good even out of what others intend for evil. Now that's a weapon of substance.

Birder's Journal

80. Teamwork

Morning Song: *Bear one another's burdens,*
and so fulfill the law of Christ
(Galatians 6:2)

Winging Through the Word
Read: Galatians 6:1-10

Thoughts on the Fly

I tried to look up the reason why Canadian Geese fly in a V-shaped formation. The first explanation I found was because it would be too hard to fly in an S. I decided look elsewhere. I eventually learned that there are two advantages to flying in V-formation. First, it conserves their energy. Each bird flies slightly ahead of the bird in front of him, resulting in less wind resistance. Birds that fly in formation can glide more often and expend less energy. Scientists have estimated that a group of 25 birds could fly 70 percent farther when flying in a V-formation than flying alone. When traveling long distances Canada Geese fly in family groups with the older birds in front and younger birds in the back. However, the front position is rotated since flying in front consumes the most energy. The birds take turns being in the front and then falling back when they get tired. This enables the geese to fly longer distances before needing to stop and rest. The second advantage to the V-formation is that it makes communication and coordination within the group much easier.

God has given similar advice to his beloved children for the same two reasons. He does not want us flying alone through life but has told us to bear each other's burdens. We are to support each other and share the load. We are to protect each other from the wind resistance of the challenges we all face. We are also to encourage and care for our spiritual leaders through prayer and through helping out in any way we can by using the spiritual gifts and talents we have been given. This will make the trip much easier for everyone especially since we are all headed to the same destination.

Birder's Journal

Morning Song: *And do not get drunk with wine…*
but be filled with the Spirit, addressing one another in
psalms and hymns and spiritual songs…
(Ephesians 5:18-19)

Winging Through the Word
Read: Ephesians 5: 1-20

Thoughts on the Fly
The first Cedar Waxwing I ever saw in the wild was on an
island not far from our camp. I had paddled to the island and
was floating in a small inlet when the pair landed in the tree
above me. They had spotted some berries and had obviously
stopped by for a quick bite. The Cedar Waxwing is stun-
ningly beautiful bird colored with a smooth and silky combination of brown, gray, and pale yellow. It has a crest on its
head, has a black mask, brilliant red "wax" marks on its wing
feathers and a yellow tip on its tail. They have several distinct
calls that sound like high-pitched trills. They are very social
birds often gathering by the hundreds to eat berries. They
are known to be voracious eaters and are especially fond of
berries. Flocks have even been seen sitting in a row on berry
bushes passing berries between each other. The one problem

Cedar Waxwings are known to have is that they apparently don't know their own limits as far as berry consumption goes. They have been known to get intoxicated on the berries. Nor do they have a designated driver policy. Whole flocks of the birds have flown drunkenly into windows and fences, some to their death.

The Scriptures encourage believers to fellowship together and to share our berries (and other possessions) like the Waxwings. While we are warned against getting drunk (designated driver, or not), that is only because God has something so much better in mind for his children than a drunken stupor. He invites us, instead, to experience the wonder of being filled with His own Spirit. And the result of that kind of filling also fills our hearts with joy and our voices with high pitched songs of praise!

Birder's Journal

82. Well Equipped

Morning Song: *Therefore take up the whole armor of God, that you may be able to withstand in the evil day, and having done all, to stand firm (Ephesians 6:13)*

Winging Through the Word
Read: Ephesians 6:10-24

Thoughts on the Fly

I looked outside the window and spotted a flock of mergansers on the lake. I called my husband to come and look. When we looked back out the window, literally seconds later, the lake was empty. "No, really," I tried to assure him, "There were mergansers out there!" Then, just as suddenly, they were back. The mergansers were out on a fishing expedition and all dived under in tandem. I was just relieved that my sanity was no longer in question. The Common Merganser is the largest of the three merganser species in North America. The male has a greenish-black crested head and upper neck, with a white breast and under parts and a black back. The female has a red tufted head and a gray body. Both have a long, narrow red bill with serrated edges formed like teeth that help them hold on to their slippery prey. That is where they get the nickname of "sawbills". They are also able to dive well below the surface to snag them. Mergansers are clearly very well designed for catching fish.

God has elegantly equipped mergansers with all they need to excel at fishing. He has equipped each of his creatures with the capabilities they need to survive and thrive. Unlike the mergansers, whose equipment is built in, he has offered each of us the freedom to opt in, or opt out of his complete equipment package. We will face a lot of challenges in this life but he has promised that if we put on his spiritual armor we will be able to stand up against every enemy and every difficult circumstance. The victory is ours because the equipment he offers is the presence of his own Spirit living inside us. That is exactly what we were designed for.

Birder's Journal

83. Adaptability

Morning Song: *Not that I am speaking of being in need, for I have learned in whatever situation I am to be content (Philippians 4:11)*

Winging Through the Word
Read: Philippians 4:4-19

Thoughts on the Fly

We were eating lunch at our favorite Jreck Sub on their deck that literally hangs over the St. Lawrence Seaway. As Bob munched on his French fries, we had the sense we were being watched. Sitting on the roof of the adjoining building was a large white seagull. When he realized he'd been spotted, he let out a loud call. I was pretty sure he was asking for a French fry. Bob set one on the rail and the seagull swooped down, grabbed and swallowed the fry and went right back to his spot. He had obviously done this before. The seagull (actually the herring gull) got its nickname because it most commonly lives by the water. They are large birds, usually gray or white, with large webbed feet. They can live almost anywhere. Being scavengers, they will eat almost anything (including French fries) and are often seen at garbage dumps sometimes in such great numbers that they have been a hazard to low flying aircraft. They have become very abundant in recent years (partly due to the abundance of garbage) so many consider them pests.

Despite their bad rap, Seagulls are beautiful and graceful in flight, and are very clever birds that can learn, remember, and even pass on behaviors. They also have the ability to drink both fresh and salt water due to a special pair of glands over their eyes that flush the salt from their systems through openings in the bill. God gave the seagulls an amazing ability to adapt to almost any environment. He has given us an even more amazing ability. When we entrust our lives to him, no matter what circumstances we find ourselves in, we can say along with Paul, "I can do all things through him who strengthens me".

Birder's Journal

84. Leap of Faith

Photo courtesy Dr. Thomas G. Barnes, USFWS

Morning Song: *Now faith is confidence in what we hope for and assurance about what we do not see (Hebrews 11:1)*

Winging Through the Word
Read: Hebrews 11:1-16

Thoughts on the Fly

On our first visit to Florida, what amazed us most was that pelicans were as common a sight down there, as seagulls are up here. And what a fascinating bird it is. There are eight different species of pelicans that live on every continent except Antarctica. It is a large bird that is best known for the pouch in its beak which the pelican uses to scoop fish out of the water. A pelican can hold up to three gallons of water in its pouch so after scooping up its meal it must first squeeze the water out the side before swallowing. Sometimes, while the pelican is draining the water, seagulls will try to steal the fish right out of its pouch. They've been known to perch on the pelican's head to reach in. The brown pelicans that we saw reach up to 48 inches long, with a seven foot wingspan. They have excellent eyesight and can spot schools of fish from as high as 50 feet. When spotted, they will dive steeply into the

167

water, often submerging completely, and capture the fish in their large throat pouches.

The Brown Pelican is the only species of pelican that makes that 50-foot plunge into the water. One might call that a leap of faith. And it is almost always rewarded with a mouth full of fish. God has called each of us to take a similar leap of faith. Like the pelican, the leap is not based on blind faith. He has given us the ability, through his Word and the gentle prompting of his Spirit, to see enough with spiritual eyes to be able to take the plunge and open our hearts to him. And that kind of leap is always rewarded with an ocean of blessings.

Birder's Journal

85. Using Their Heads

Morning Song: *Count it all joy, my brothers, when you meet trials of various kinds, for you know that the testing of your faith produces steadfastness* (James 1:2, 3)

Winging Through the Word
Read: James 1:1-18

Thoughts on the Fly

I watched a steady stream of chickadees land on my hand, grab a sunflower seed, and dart away. I used to think they did that just to allow the next customer a turn. While I can't totally rule out politeness, I have since learned that chickadees have a much more practical reason for taking the seeds to an alternate location. Black-capped chickadees commonly store or "cache" the food they gather in multiple locations to help them get through the winter months. Chickadees are also known for their innate ability to remember where each of their caches is. Researchers have discovered that the hippocampus (brain) is larger in birds that cache food than in closely related species that do not. One study compared the hippocampus of chickadees in Alaska (where caching is a critical factor in a bird's survival) with those of chickadees collected in Colorado (where it is less important). The brains of the Alaskan chickadees were significantly larger than those of Colorado birds in spite of the fact that the overall sizes of the birds were larger in the Colorado populations.

So, it appears to be because of the challenging environment that the chickadee's brain grows larger and gains a greater capacity to function. That is a principle one could apply to almost every area of life. The Bible tells us that God can use the trials in our lives to produce a godly character. And even more, he has promised to work all things – even the bad things – together for the good in the lives of his beloved children. So, when those inevitable difficulties come we can use our brains to remember his promises and his faithfulness to us in the past and allow him to use them to make us "perfect and complete, lacking in nothing".

Birder's Journal

86. All Kinds of Words

Morning Song: *All kinds of animals, birds, reptiles and sea creatures are being tamed and have been tamed by mankind (James 3:7)*

Winging Through the Word
Read: James 3:1-18

Thoughts on the Fly

His name is Ziggy. And he could tell you that, himself. My friend, among her menagerie of pets, has a lovely and very personable parrot named Ziggy. From what she has told me, he is quite the conversationalist. Knowing how much my friend likes to talk, I wasn't too surprised that her parrot had picked up so many words from her. But Ziggy has also learned to bark (my friend has three dogs, too). Parrots, along with ravens, crows, and magpies, are among the most intelligent birds. But their ability to imitate human voices is what makes parrots so popular as pets. There are over 350 different parrot species though most of them are native exclusively to the tropics. Parrots are often very brightly colored, have curved bills, strong legs and clawed feet with four toes on each foot, two pointing forward and two pointing backward. Some parrot species can live for over 80 years. What parrots are probably best known for is that if trained properly they can mimic human speech. Some species have mastered a vocabulary of almost two thousand words.

My friend would be the first to tell you what great pets parrots make. It is amazing to me that God has given humankind the capacity to tame and train some of his other creatures. The Apostle James compared creatures that people could tame with the human tongue that so many of us can't. I'm not referring to friends or birds that talk a lot but those who use their speech in ways that hurt others and offend the Lord. But James's point wasn't to discourage us. Rather, it was to remind us that the God who created the tongue will fill us with words of wisdom and peace when we commit our speech to him.

Birder's Journal

87. Obsessed

Morning Song: *Like newborn infants, long for the pure spiritual milk, that by it you may grow up to salvation—if indeed you have tasted that the Lord is good (1 Peter 2:2-3)*

Winging Through the Word
Read: Psalm 34:1-22

Thoughts on the Fly

I heard the familiar hammering sound and spotted the same bird busy at work on the same tree. He had made a vertical line of holes on the tree and showed no interest in stopping. Being a little worried about the tree, I tried to scare him away, but he was back as soon as I walked away. One might say that he seemed to be obsessed with pecking holes in our tree. I discovered that our passionate percussionist was a yellow-bellied sapsucker. The yellow-bellied sapsucker is a medium-sized woodpecker with a black and white back. It is aptly named with its pale yellow underside, and its taste for tree sap. It is the only woodpecker that pecks small squarish holes in straight lines down a tree trunk to obtain sap which it laps up with its brush-like tongue. They also eat the insects attracted to the sapwells.

I watched our sapsucker's nonstop performance with fascination as he continued to drill holes and suck sap just as God designed him to do. God designed humans to be united with him. As Blaise Pascal put it, "There is a God shaped vacuum in the heart of every man which cannot be filled by any created thing, but only by God, the Creator, made known through Jesus". Once the sapsucker gets a taste of sap, he becomes obsessed with getting more. We are told to "Taste and see that the LORD is good; blessed is the one who takes refuge in him" (Psalm 34:8). Once we get a taste of God's great love for us, we are told that we will "long for the pure spiritual milk" that will enable us to deepen our relationship with him. Some of us might even seem obsessed in our passion for worshiping our Creator.

Birder's Journal

Photo courtesy MDF

Morning Song: *But you are a chosen race, a royal priesthood, a holy nation, a people for his own possession, that you may proclaim the excellencies of him who called you out of darkness into his marvelous light (1 Peter 2:9)*

Winging Through the Word
Read: 1 Peter 2:1-12

Thoughts on the Fly
I picked one of the largest sunflowers in our garden and hung it on top of the bird feeder. I soon heard a loud "jay jay" call and spotted a large blue jay hard at work pecking at the fresh seeds. The blue jay is a member of the crow family that stands between nine and twelve inches tall. In addition to their own noisy calls, blue jays are known to mimic the sound of hawks possibly to inform other jays that a hawk is in the area, or to trick other birds into believing that a hawk is nearby. The blue jay is best known for its bright blue color on its upper parts, pale gray underparts, a black necklace, wings and tail with black and white patches, and a blue head crest. That said, blue jays are not really blue! Their feathers

175

appear as blue, but they are actually black. The bright blue color is the result of the unique inner structure of the feathers that refract the light and make it look blue. Refracted light is pretty much the same science that explains why the sky is blue.

It is interesting that light can have that kind of effect on the color of a bird. It turned a rather plain black bird into something strikingly beautiful. One might compare the refraction of light on the blue jay to how those who love the Lord reflect his light to the world. We are just common sinners like everyone else. Not much to look at. But when the Light of the World enters our lives we are transformed into children of the light. We are called to shine that light—the light of Jesus—to a world lost in darkness and when we do, it is strikingly beautiful.

Birder's Journal

89. Peace on Earth

Morning Song: *"Then I saw a new heaven and a new earth, for the first heaven and the first earth had passed away, and the sea was no more"*
(Revelations 21:1)

Winging Through the Word
Read: Isaiah 65:17-25

Thoughts on the Fly
I looked out the window, almost contentedly, at our eight birdfeeders. It was a sunny day and there were different kinds of birds at almost all eight of them at the same time. We had gold finches at the finch feeder, hummingbirds at the hummingbird feeder, woodpeckers and a blue jay taking turns on the two suet feeders. Mr. Cardinal was happily dining on the safflower on the main feeder while the Mrs., along with almost a dozen juncos and sparrows nibbled on seeds that had fallen on the ground. It was an extraordinarily colorful and animated scene not to mention the concert of beautiful songs that could put a symphony to shame.

It struck me how well all our little bird friends got along sharing such a small space. Oh, that the rest of the world could learn from them. Then we truly would have peace on earth. But the peacefulness and beauty of the scene before me was a small reminder that one day we will. People, animals, birds, and in fact all of creation will live in perfect harmony. There will be no more war, no more sorrow or tears. Jesus promised each of us his peace now and peace for all the earth when he returns. He said, "Peace I leave with you; my peace I give to you. Not as the world gives do I give to you. Let not your hearts be troubled, neither let them be afraid . . . I am going away, and I will come to you . . ." (John 14:27,28). The new heaven and the new earth will be a place of perfect peace because the Prince of Peace will return to establish his kingdom. For now, I will enjoy my lovely little bird sanctuary. Though, it wouldn't hurt to add one more feeder.

Birder's Journal

90. Never Far Away

Morning Song: *And I heard a loud voice from the throne saying, "Behold, the dwelling place of God is with man. He will dwell with them, and they will be his people, and God himself will be with them as their God"*
(Revelations 21:3)

Winging Through the Word
Read: Revelations 22:1-21

Thoughts on the Fly
Summer was almost over. I kayaked over to take one last look at the eagle's nest. It had been empty the past several times I had visited. I figured the young ones had left the nest and the family had moved on for the season. As I headed back home I looked over my shoulder one last time and to my delight I spotted the mother eagle perched at the top of one of the tallest trees on the island. She hadn't left yet after all. Which obviously meant that the young eagles hadn't left either. While the eagle parents will not leave the young eaglets, they *will* give them a little space to allow them to learn to survive on their own. Though they will intentionally have little contact with the young birds, they are never far

away. As the young birds watch their parents hunt and fish, they will learn to do the same by practicing. But even in the learning stage, the parents will still occasionally feed them until they are ready to make it on their own. In time, they too will learn to hunt and to soar.

The day will come when we will soar away from this earth to a better place—a heavenly place. In the mean time, we have a Heavenly Father who is never far away. He is ever present and keeping his watchful eye on each of his children. Whether we are consciously aware of his presence or not, God is there. He has assured us. "…I will never leave you nor forsake you" (Heb 13:5). That's a promise. But like the mother eagle, he allows us to learn to walk by faith until the day that we can fly away on eagle's wings, to spend eternity with him.

Birder's Journal

Made in the USA
Middletown, DE
23 April 2015